The Twig of Revelation

*Dedicated to
Miriam and Susan
for their constant encouragement
and support.*

HAROLD VAN COLLE

The Twig of Revelation

*Understanding Paranormal & Normal Experiences
– A True Account of an Extraordinary Adventure*

ASHGROVE PRESS, BATH

Published in Great Britain by
ASHGROVE PRESS LIMITED
Bath Road, Norton St Philip,
Bath, BA3 6LW

© Harold Van Colle 1997

First published 1997

ISBN 1–85398–101–X

Photoset by Ann Buchan (Typesetters), Middlesex
Printed and bound in Great Britain by
Redwood Books, Trowbridge, Wilts

Contents

PART III   *Current Reflections*

Prologue

Long ago I decided that there was no point in asking 'why was I born?'. I know how and where my birth occurred, but not why I, or any other human being was put on this planet. The only question worth asking, I feel, is 'now that I am here, which is the best way to live my life?' My conclusion was, and still is, that to be of some sort of help to my fellow human beings is a philosophy worth going for, because I have found that if I succeed in creating some degree of happiness in another person, then I become happier myself. Being fully aware of how self-righteous this sounds does not deter me from continuing in that way because, if I consider an alternative, for example, being inconsiderate or selfish, leading to the unhappiness of others, then the result for me would be my own unhappiness.

However, I am aware, also, of the fact that if I am unable to help myself, then it might be difficult, sometimes, to be of help to others. It must be recognised that in this world there seems to be an increasing number of unhappy people, and there are many reasons for that situation. Many books could be written, and debates held, as to what those reasons might be. One particular reason has to be, as a generalisation, that the human brain, 'the machine' involved in everything that one does or does not do, is being used very badly. The 'Machine' has great potential capability, but is being badly programmed. To some extent this state of affairs can be attributed to unsatisfactory family life, the abandonment of the essence of most religions (not the rituals, but the guidelines for living), the use of scientific devices as an alternative to using the brain more actively, the effect of the media, including radio and television, the misconception that pleasure is synonymous with 'happiness', materialism and indulgence in various forms of drugs, including alcohol and tobacco, and the lack of purpose in life leading to the absence of any feelings of fulfilment.

I know that I am unable to suggest any one way of life, or any particular activity which, if adopted, would be the universal panacea for unhappy people. Each person has to discover his or her own Shangri-la, and then only by being prepared to engage in voyages of discovery. That brings me to the reason I have written this book. I do know that as I start I find the task quite daunting. Nevertheless I have put a stream of questions to myself and have reached the conclusion that some readers might find it both interesting and helpful, helpful insofar as it might inspire some to go on their own adventures. This book is about a true adventure of mine which started over 28 years ago and is still going on. It can never end for me, but the discoveries I made were of tremendous value and help to me, and have been instrumental in helping thousands of others who came to me seeking help. Those many people were never told by me what to do, nor what not to do. All I did, and still do, was to share with them the knowledge and understanding gained from my adventure. Knowledge and understanding, especially of one's own brain-mind system, become the basis for wisdom. Without that system in operation, nothing would exist for an individual.

My adventure started because of an event which occurred by sheer chance. The effect of this trivial event was most profound. It was as if I had been affected by the touch of a 'power' from somewhere. I did not put any religious interpretation upon what took place nor upon what followed as the result. All I know is that I was 'propelled', for lack of a better word, into starting the most exciting adventure of my life. In writing this book I hope, most sincerely, that it will inspire some readers to become more adventurous, especially in the use of their brains, to become less concerned about what others might think of them, and ultimately to experience the feeling of fulfilment. That in turn would provide some justification for being on this planet. The book is divided into three parts. Part I covers the first three years of the most intense activity of my life, and Part II covers the following 25 years. The reader should bear in mind that the initial activities gave rise to thoughts, theories, and opinions which have undergone all kinds of change and modification as time passed, coupled with ongoing experiences. However, I relate events as they occurred, and how I thought about them at the time. Part III has enabled me to put on record a few of the countless reflections which continue to pass through my mind from time to time.

PART I

The First Three Years

1: The Event

I have been involved in many activities in life including chiropody, pharmacy, export, philately, postal history, numismatics, archaeology, art and music, both in professional and amateur ways. What a mixture! However, I have found that all activities, whether maintained or transitory, whether successful or otherwise, are a source of knowledge and experience and, for my part, have a common thread – learning about people and about oneself. Furthermore, there must be things within a human being which influence an individual. Atonal people do not respond well to musical sounds; the artistic often are not good at mathematics or science.

Of all my activities one in particular – numismatics – gave rise to the event which changed the course of my life. I was involved as a collector-dealer in the coins of the Ancient Britons and Anglo-Saxons. I attended auctions and they were a great source of learning about human behaviour. I also visited clients in their homes and gave displays at exhibitions. It was during an exhibition that I was approached by a farmer who happened to be a keen collector and student of the coins of the Ancient Britons, including pre-Roman times. He lived in a part of the country where these particular coins were to be found on the seashore, especially after stormy seas had lashed the cliffs, and was known for his particular interest by some locals who would bring coins to him as and when they found them. Naturally they were rewarded for their labours. In addition, when walking in or around his ploughed fields he would come across further artefacts of the Romano-

British period such as pins, buckles and coins. He collected and studied them, but was frustrated by the fact that these items only surfaced when the land had been ploughed. If only, he thought, he could find an instrument or device by which he could detect the presence of these metal objects in the ground.

Because of our common interest in coins our friendship grew, and he told me of his wish to find a satisfactory metal detector. He was aware of some on the market, but they were unsatisfactory in two respects: firstly they could not penetrate soil more than a few inches and, secondly, covered only a few square inches of surface at a time. It would take more than a lifetime to investigate one field. Had I any knowledge of any more satisfactory instrument? As already mentioned, one of my previous activities was export, and in addition to my scientific background as a pharmacist, I also happened to export scientific instruments, so had connections in that field. I promised my farmer friend that I would make some enquiries and report back.

My enquiries 'in the trade' produced no more than information about various unsatisfactory electric metal detectors, with one exception – an expensive device about which the manufacturers could offer no explanation as to why or how it worked. In brief, it consisted of a pair of metal rods about 24 inches long, each with a handle at the end at right angles to the rod, the rods being attached to the handles by means of bearings which allowed the rods to swing left and right. Attached to one of the handles was a gadget holding a series of 'samples' such as iron, carbon, pottery, water, etc. The idea was to attach a finger to one of the 'samples', then hold the rods in front, horizontal to the ground, and about 10 inches apart. By walking forward the rods would move if one approached some metal or other object – according to which 'sample' had been touched. In general the rods tended to move inwards towards each other as a substance being sought was 'detected'.

The manufacturers were kind enough to lend me a pair of rods in the hope of export prospects. I tried them out, and whilst I did notice some rod movements when I traversed drains or other large subterranean structures, they would not give me anything like a satisfactory reaction in respect of a penny lying on the ground, having previously scattered quite a few. The outcome was that by buying a couple of lengths of ordinary round iron rods about a quarter of an inch thick and approximately 32 inches long, and bending each rod about 8 inches from the end at right angles (to form the equivalent of a handle), the results I obtained were similar to those obtained with the expensive ones, for the outlay of a few pence. Although results were not as I had wished, I was nevertheless intrigued by the fact that something of an unusual nature did occur.

The next meeting with my farmer friend was at an hotel in Piccadilly, during which I told him of my efforts and results. So far as the rods were concerned, he said, the idea was very old. In his part of the country they had used bent knitting needles for seeking drains and water. The method was well known to country folk, but did not solve the problem of finding small metal objects. He said the method was called 'dowsing' or 'divining', for which one could use the forked twig, and as we were in Piccadilly near to Green Park, he suggested we go into the park, find a forked twig and use it to seek, say, water.

Into the park we went, and when there was no park keeper in sight, he found a forked twig on a tree and broke it off. Holding a limb of the twig in each hand he proceeded to walk around the grass until, in quite a short time, I saw him struggling with the twig, the point of which seemed to insist upon going upwards. I expressed my doubts about what I was seeing. He suggested that I try it for myself. This I did, but nothing happened. He suggested that the twig might be too thick and that a more slender one might be more suitable for me. This slender version led to no reactions either. It was, it seemed, a waste of time, and I remained sceptical.

Being my wife's birthday, I had arranged for her and other members of my family to pick me up at the hotel in Piccadilly, as we were all going to a cinema in Leicester Square. My wife arrived with an evening newspaper under her arm, so I tucked the twig inside the fold of the paper, and said goodbye to my farmer friend. We made our way to Leicester Square and joined a queue for tickets outside the cinema. In this situation my wife had time to express her curiosity about my meeting with the farmer, so I removed the twig from the paper to show her how it was supposed to be held. While holding it in the pre-scribed manner the queue started to move forward – and the twig shot up in my hands!!! It was as if I had been touched by some power which overwhelmed me.

What I have reported so far happened over 28 years ago, but the details are accurate because I kept a very precise record of all these events. But even without those written records I shall never be able to forget the event. As to the date, I always associate it with my wife's birthday.

The outcome of this event was that I immediately abandoned all activities in order to devote myself to finding out why this phenomenon had occurred. My initial 'devotion to the cause' lasted three years, full time, seven days a week from morning till night. As my wife remembered the farmer's reference to the bent rods or knitting needles as being used for what he called 'dowsing' or 'divining', she went to the local library and found a book for me on the elements of dowsing. In this book reference was made to the use of a pendulum, and that device seemed to be more favoured than the rods and twig. So I took myself off to a bookshop near Charing Cross Road specialising in the 'unusual', and was able to purchase a black plastic pendulum. Following the suggestions in the book, I set out to master it. After two full days with it swinging and gyrating I felt I might go insane, but it was only through my wife's encouragement that I did not abandon the whole project. I continued experimenting with the pendulum for a further day, and by the end of that day I began to feel that it was behaving in a more meaningful way. However, I developed a growing feeling that reading the book on dowsing was giving rise to problems. Expectation or prediction of the pendulum's movement led to the occurrence of the expectation. So I abandoned all reading about dowsing and proceeded to experiment on the basis of logical progression from one observation to another – a kind of extrapolation.

The pendulum's oscillations or rotations were not due to any deliberate movement of my hand but were, nevertheless, the result of a seemingly involuntary muscular movement. The pendulum certainly did nothing if not held in my hand.

In the course of almost obsessive experimenting I discovered that by my thought only I could make the pendulum oscillate in any direction I willed it, or rotate clockwise or anti-clockwise, or remain still. Never was it necessary for me to move my hand deliberately. In fact the movements my hand was making were so small that it was obvious that the pendulum was merely the means of amplifying those tiny movements. I discovered, subsequently, that this movement of muscles in response to thoughts was well known as 'ideo-motor' activity.

But ideo-motor activity was only the beginning of the story. Still experimenting, I discovered that the pendulum, and of course my hand, could move for reasons other than deliberate or ideo-motor. It moved towards anything I might be seeking. If I placed several objects on a table, each made of a different material, for example a penny, a pebble, a cup and a flower, and then maintained a thought about any one of those items, the pendulum would swing towards the one I was thinking of. The story did not end there. I found the pendulum gave responses to almost anything thinkable. For example I could think about the date of manufacture of an object, electricity, water, bones, cavities, etc. The pendulum, also the rods and forked twig, gave some response to all such items and many more. Again, for example, while looking at a person while holding the pendulum it became possible to engage in what was equivalent to medical diagnosis by thinking about various parts or organs of the body. If the part or organ was healthy then the pendulum would oscillate towards the person, but if unhealthy, damaged or diseased, then the pendulum would not swing towards the person. It would swing at an angle or would start to gyrate.

Over several months I found I became riveted, as it were, to the pendulum's movements, having discovered they could be related to foreign languages, radio-activity and heaven knows what else, but always in connection with my brain-mind system. So now I had established that there was a direct relationship between the mind and the body in physiological terms, movement being physiological. The implications were, and still are, enormous in relation to almost every aspect of human activity.

2: *Unstoppable*

With each new observation or discovery my interest grew and I reached a further conclusion. Not only was there a direct relationship between my brain-mind system and my body, but there was also a relationship between the thought of a substance or force (e.g. electricity) and the actual substance or force. This I found by using, at first, the bent rods to detect water, electricity, gas, bones etc. There was however a flaw. The flaw was unreliability. In scientific experiments one can deal with substances or forces with pre-determined constants (temperature, pressure, humidity, weight, and so on). Where my experiments were concerned, I could not arrange for my brain-mind system to be in a constant state, hence the scientific method could not be applied. The relationship between the experimenter and the observed object tended to break down – subsequently confirmed by an eminent researcher.

So now I observed that there was a kind of mental contest between expectation and a situation of no-expectation one way or another, the latter situation not easy to achieve if a person has an analytical mind. And if someone with a scientific background were to ask me to demonstrate any phenomenon as proof, under what scientists call 'controlled' conditions, usually things went wrong because of my anxiety about not wishing to fail. But even this situation taught me something important (failure itself is a great teacher) – that if a person wills something, to do something, but at the same time harbours doubts about his or her ability to achieve, the doubt is a negative thought and acts physiologically in opposition to what the person wishes to achieve. So this gave me a new slant to the interpretation, in physiological terms, to words such as 'try', 'determination' and 'hope', especially in situations where the only requirement would have been a simple and sincere decision to do or not do something. To include the words try, determination or hope would probably lead to failure. This last observation gave new meaning to the cliche 'positive thinking'. In most everyday situations it does NOT mean 'be more positive'. It simply means making a decision and removing all negative thoughts about the decision before putting it into practice. If there is no negative one does not need to be more positive. Just be decisive. I found that if a decision in those circumstances does not work out as wished, then the experience becomes a source of learning. When conducting experiments I found that I always learnt more from seeking the reasons for failure than from being

19

successful. Of course the words try, determination and hope are valid in situations involving opposition to what one decides, or when a situation is beyond one's control.

The pendulum, bent rods and forked twig were my constant companions, and my mind worked overtime, always looking for new avenues to explore. I really was anxious to prove that dowsing was factual, and hit upon the idea that archaeology might prove the answer. I could not know what was actually in the ground, nor the whereabouts of a buried object, in advance. So I obtained permission from my local council, and also from the lessee of the land, who had a herd of cows, to dig on some open 'green belt' space, using my various devices, plus my brain-mind system, to seek, for example, pottery and bones. Apart from the interference of the cows from time to time (they seemed to be filled with curiosity and always surrounded me wherever I was working), my digging proved very interesting. With the aid of my rods I obtained reactions from pieces of pottery, tiles and bones, depending upon what I had decided in my mind to seek, and then, with the aid of a very efficient spade and trowel, I proceeded to dig where the reactions had taken place to see whether the pottery or bones were, in fact, where the rods had reacted. My own garden was not far from the open space, so at weekends I dug up areas of grass and flower beds, aided by members of the local historical society. We were rewarded by finding fragments of pottery of the 13th to 14th centuries, verified by a Government Ancient Monuments department, which are now in a local museum. Pieces of glass, clay pipes, tiles and other artefacts came to light in the course of time.

Now something quite unusual occurred. Having spent a few days by the sea, with my wife and sister, we were en route home and happened to stop at an antique shop. In the course of conversation with the proprietor it was suggested that an archaeological site on my route might prove of interest. So off we went and found the site near a local village, where there were the remains of an old priory in a meadow adjoining a farm. The lady house-keeper gave me permission to go on to the site, but it was October, and the archaeological group responsible for it had finished operations for the year. But as I had told her I was a dowser, she said she would like me to meet the farmer, who would be home at lunchtime. So we walked over the site, seeing some stone foundations, and with nothing in particular in mind I held my rods, and also the pendulum.

Then the farmer arrived, and during a brief chat he suggested 'find them a body – they have not found any-thing of interest lately'. 'They' referred to the archaeological group. Laughingly I said I would do my best to find a body. Off we went back to the site and decided to look for 'bones' with the aid of my pendulum. At this point I should mention that the archaeological group had worked on the site for 13 years, and had drawn up a more or less complete plan of the priory. They had excavated almost every nook and cranny. Nevertheless I continued my search for 'bones', and the pendulum kept oscillating in a very definite direction, eventually leading me to an area which was covered with sifted earth and grass seed. My pendulum directed me to about the centre of the sifted earth area, and eventually by going back and forth I was able to mark out an area of approximately 7 feet by 4 feet by means of wooden stakes at the corners with string in between. Of course there were no bones to be seen, nor any evidence of their existence. Furthermore it was quite obvious that this particular area had had the recent atten-tion of the archaeologists. In marking out the 7 feet by 4 feet I got the feeling that these bones were surrounded by a 'wall'. I hastened to inform the farmer, who said it was fortunate that I was there that day because the leader of the archaeological group was coming to a museum in the village that same afternoon, and he would arrange for me to meet him at the museum. And so it happened, and I

21

What the pendulum found that the archaeologists missed

persuaded a sceptical archaeologist to come with me back to the site. On arrival, seeing the area I had staked out, he was quick to point out that the area in question had been excavated recently and had proved to be archaeologically barren: hence the sifted earth and grass seed.

Quite undeterred, even though a little apprehensive, I asked his permission to re-dig the limited staked out area, because it was important for me as a proof or otherwise of dowsing. After all I was quite prepared to do the digging. In short, he agreed and said I would find spades and buckets in the nearby barn. Aided by my wife and sister we dug feverishly, and lo and behold, eventually a row of small red tiles came into view. But the light was fading, so digging had to be postponed, and it was agreed I could return the next day and continue. It was about two hours drive from the site to home, but never mind, we were back on the job early next day. By the end of that day, again with light fading, we had removed an enormous amount of soil and clay to expose a thick stone coffin, without a lid, which seemed to be filled with clay, and with a few small tiles around the edge. The coffin was also hollowed out at one end, as if to take a head. Before leaving I claimed the right to probe the clay with a small stick at the hollowed out end, and was more than interested to find that it stopped after sinking into the clay about two or three inches. But the light failed, and the final act had to be postponed until the next morning.

When we arrived at the site the next day we found that news of the find had got around, and that some villagers with usual curiosity, plus a local doctor, were already there. We gently removed the top layer of clay to reveal a complete skeleton, with the skull, as anticipated, occupying the hollowed out end of the coffin. I felt I had triumphed in the cause of dowsing. Why had not the archaeological group found it? Because, confessed the archaeologist, they had not dug deep enough. One more observation – the position of the coffin was within about three inches from the line predicted on the surface of the soil. The accuracy was incredible. This event was thoroughly and independently investigated by scientists associated with a society of psychical research, and they stated it was probably the best example of dowsing ever recorded. The reader should note that, contrary to popular belief, dowsing is not limited to finding water.

However there was much more to this event than simply the excitement of finding a skeleton in a stone coffin. A question arose in my mind. The coffin was made of a type of stone common to that part of the country, and there were many lumps of the stone in the soil around the area where the coffin was found. The question was, therefore, why did not the pendulum give a reaction to these pieces of stone before the area of the coffin was reached? Ultimately the answer came to mind. Quite obviously the large mass of the stone coffin, also the larger quantity of the bones, dominated the area. This observation became a cornerstone in my understanding of how the brain works: the principle of 'domination'.

Here was another example of how a seemingly unimportant, even though spectacular, event had enormous importance in understanding human behaviour in everyday life. I will return to this matter later. Meanwhile it is worth reporting that while dowsing in the area of the skeleton in the coffin – probably that of one of the priors – I obtained pendulum reactions indicating that there were several more lots of bones in the area. I told the archaeologist exactly where those reactions had occurred, and the sequel was that when digging resumed the following year, several more skeletons, not in coffins, were found exactly where indicated.

3: More Logic and Extrapolation

As can be imagined, the experience of finding the skeleton and coffin was enormously exciting as an event, but I had to remind myself constantly why I was involved in these activities, that is to say why the twig, rods and pendulum did what they did. Or, more to the point, what was the significance of the movements of my hands which activated the various dowsing devices. Why, I asked myself, did the pendulum swing towards what I was seeking?

When people spoke of what is popularly called the occult' or, sometimes, 'the supernatural', it always gave rise to an uneasy reaction in my mind, quite a powerful one. After all, I reasoned, anything that occurs in Nature must of necessity be called natural, even though a particular event might be described as being strange, unusual or certainly not conforming to the everyday experiences of the average person.

Therefore, because I regard Nature, or the forces of Nature, as a source of wonder, and know that most things in Nature, especially living things – plants, animals and humans – have certain abilities, I can only conclude that those abilities, even strange or unusual ones, must have been organised by Nature for a purpose. What was the purpose of the moving hand? Was, I pondered, the movement limited to just hands? These were questions that refused to remain unanswered. So it occurred to me to consider what, in Nature's creations, could be considered as the priority. I reached the conclusion that survival was probably paramount, and therefore many of the phenomena I had observed were connected with survival mechanisms. After all, if Nature took the trouble to create the vast range of living things, there would be no purpose in such creations if Nature did not also provide the opportunity, if not a guarantee, for a period of survival.

25

As this seemed logical, I had to validate my survival hypothesis by considering actual examples in Nature. Not very difficult, I found. Take seeds and plants for example. Roots grow towards water in the soil, or store water in thick leaves to be able to survive drought. Plants move or turn towards light, as is well known in botany. Seeds often have hard outer coverings to protect them from drought, or from being damaged when eaten by birds, another survival of the species mechanism. Animals walk towards water when they need it and when they can detect it via their normal senses. In drought, an animal is unaware of the whereabouts of water, but is nevertheless very thirsty. Its brain must be dominated by the physiological need for water. I feel that in such circumstances the animal is 'led' by 'automatic walking' towards a source of water, even though there would be no guarantee that the animal would necessarily survive the journey.

When a dowser is seeking water he organises his brain to think the word 'water' and maintains the thought of that word. His pendulum will then swing in the direction of water. The dowser is organising his brain to become dominated by either the word 'water', or a mental picture of water. This was my hypothesis. I had to consider finding some further supporting evidence.

Some time after locating the skeleton on the site of the priory, I returned to the farm just for an outing and to see whether further excavations had taken place. To my surprise I found that the farm had been sold to a younger farmer who seemed to know all about my previous activities as a dowser. The archaeological group was no longer active on the site, which was gradually being incorporated into the farm. However, the young farmer, and his young manager, were interested to know more about dowsing, especially as they wanted to locate land drains in the fields. It so happened I did not have my dowsing devices with me. That proved fortunate because it led me to suggest to the young farmer (not his manager – he was very sceptical about the whole business) that he should dowse for the land drains without any device to help him. So I suggested that he should stand in a field, quite relaxed, with his arms hanging limply at his side, and maintain thoughts of both water and land drains. I gave him no idea of what possible reactions might take place. He stood, with eyes shut, and commenced his thinking process. In a short while his left arm started to float upwards towards his left, of its own accord, away from his body, followed shortly afterwards by his right arm floating upwards, also towards his left, across his chest. Thus both arms were pointing leftwards. Unexpectedly both his feet started to twist themselves towards the left, followed by the rest of his body, so that eventually his body was now facing the direction of his arms which were now directly in front of him, raised and still pointing in the same original direction.

What then happened left the farmer's manager virtually dumbstruck. There were the farmer's legs moving themselves forward as if he were a zombie, and causing him to walk but not as a deliberate act. Needless to say I would not allow this one event to become my only source of conviction that my hypothesis about animals in drought was correct. I formulated countless experiments with many people, known in psychology as 'naive' (no person having any fore-knowledge). I can assure the reader that I had no wish to lead myself up 'a blind alley', nor to attempt to deceive myself in any way. I continued to experiment over the years, and do so even to this day, to make sure that any hypothesis is sound.

The adventure in which I was now totally, absolutely, and almost helplessly involved, led me to make an endless series of approaches from various angles, in order to clarify and make meaningful every experience and every thought that crossed my mind. In fact I now began to give more serious thought to the idea of 'mind'. I accepted as fact that I had a brain, but what was the mind? – a word used so frequently yet so little understood. Some psychologists, and others, do not even believe that there is such a thing as a mind.

I was indeed fortunate to have, in my circle of friends, some with sound scientific backgrounds. Some were very sceptical about my involvements, others more open-minded and interested. But all were useful in the role of 'the devil's advocate'. I was not allowed to get away with anything. One friend, a psychiatrist, was particularly co-operative, as also was a Professor of Psychology with whom I had a very lengthy correspondence.

4: *Mental Telepathy*

Following my observations from dowsing, it suddenly dawned on me that if a thought of a substance resulted in my brain (if not my consciousness) having knowledge of the whereabouts of the actual substance, then there must be some relationship between a real substance and a thought of it. I have not yet resolved that matter – it nags my mind incessantly. I comfort myself by considering, as a truth, the possibility that Nature, the Creator, did not intend humans to know everything. After all, if scientists were to understand everything, they would be the equivalent of Nature or God. I have yet to see a scientist create even one blade of grass.

If a relationship does exist between a substance and a thought of that substance, and it seems to be so, then it must represent some form of mental telepathy. Here I will relate an amusing experience. During the most active time of my three years intensive research, I would always be found holding either a pendulum or the bent metal rods. And so it was one day that a man from the Water Board came to my house to see about some water problem that I had notified. As he walked in he noticed my metal rods and said 'What are you doing with those?'. I explained my interest in dowsing, and he responded 'I have been using rods like those for the past twelve years to track the water mains into houses, but I never let my mates see me. They would laugh at me.' I enquired how he had learnt to use such rods, and he told me that an 'old chap' at the Water Board used them for 40 years and had shown him how to do it. I also heard from a surveyor attached to the local council that he used rods to track underground pipes and cables on demolition sites. Further enquiries led to hearing from the head of the local Parks Division of the council that he used similar rods to find land drains.

Now there is something particularly interesting in these reports. For example, when the man from the Water Board was trying to locate the water mains pipe in the ground, he would, of course, walk over ground where there was likely to be the gas and electricity mains supply, and because he is only thinking 'water', he gets no reaction with the rods when passing over the gas and electricity mains. It would occur over one or other of the latter if his maintained thought had been either 'gas' or electricity', in which event he would get no reaction when walking over the water mains pipe. I, and friends who found they had dowsing ability (and quite a high percentage of people have the ability), checked and re-checked countless times the facts just reported, and have been able to confirm those findings.

Once in this field of mental and physical activity, one begins to feel almost overwhelmed by logic which, without mercy, gives rise to an almost endless stream of further ideas and experiments which I felt compelled to pursue. And so it was that having considered the relationship between thought and a substance, I now had to consider the possibility of mental telepathy between one person and another. The one thing that the experiments with water, gas and electricity had shown was that there was, apparently, no physical force, in truly scientific terms, that impinges upon a dowser's mind, when actively dowsing, that will cause an involuntary reaction. The dowser seems to be blocking out everything except the one thing or substance he is seeking. Scientists get worried about so-called 'forces' which cannot be measured and quantified.

So far as mental telepathy from person to person is concerned, I will tell what happened when a psychiatrist friend offered to help me in two ways. Firstly he agreed to be my guinea-pig and, secondly, he allowed me access to an electroencephalograph (E.E.G.) – a machine used for recording brain activity. So on the appointed day we met, and he volunteered to lay relaxed on a hospital bed, his head wired up to the E.E.G. by means of special electrodes. The E.E.G. was under the control of an assistant.

My objective was to try, by mental telepathy, to affect my friend's brain to an extent that would show an irrefutable recording on the E.E.G. paper. If I could do just that, it would be the answer to all the sceptical scientists. That's how I saw it. However, hopes and wishes are not always fulfilled, and so it was that after about one hour of trying one thought after another, with no obvious response showing on the recording paper, the assistant suggested that after just one more go, the session should end, because there was a mountain of the E.E.G. recording paper on the floor. I am not sure why, but this time, for my last experiment, I decided to do something that I had not done previously. I wrote on a piece of paper what my thought would be, and gave it to the assistant for future reference. What I wrote was: 'Your nose is itching, scratch it'.

The E.E.G. machine was in an ante-room with a clear glass screen, so I left that room and took up a position next to my wired-up friend who was lying completely relaxed with his eyes closed, and started thinking about making his nose itch by telepathy. I thought and thought with intensity (after all, this was going to be my last chance), and after maintaining my thought for about two minutes I got a signal from the assistant, through the glass screen, that there was no apparent change in the recording, and that she was going to switch off the machine. Having done so, she called out to my friend, who was still laying with his eyes closed, that the experiment had ended and that he could now open his eyes. He duly opened them and sat upright, immediately followed by a vigorous rubbing of his nose. I asked him whether it was one of his usual habits to rub his nose. 'No', he said. Then 'why did you do it?' I asked. 'Because it was itching' he replied. 'Was it itching while you were laying with your eyes closed?' I asked. 'Yes', he said. 'Then why didn't you rub it then?' I asked. 'Because I didn't want to spoil your experiment' was his wonderful reply. I can assure the reader I lost no time in showing him the written record of my last thought, and the E.E.G. lady and I did a celebratory dance. What a cliff-hanger!

But telepathy experiments did not stop there. After all, I conjectured, if I could make a person's nose itch by telepathy, what else could I do by the same method? I am sure the reader will have no difficulty in imagining the range of possibilities that crossed my mind. Here is a brief report of just a few of the very many experiments I conducted, but always using people who had no prior knowledge of what would or might happen:

- someone's toothache was alleviated by simply looking at the person and thinking 'anti-pain' for a couple of minutes.
- many headaches were dealt with in the same way.
- two scientific observers brought a lady to me (previously not known to me), no reason having been given to her for the visit except that it was for an experiment, and I hypnotised her from another room.

31

- I instructed a few mothers of children not older than three years how to use their thoughts to overcome bedwetting. I published a report and other practitioners used the same method and reported quite a high success rate.
- I managed to influence a young lady friend to 'conduct an orchestra', by telepathic thought. She had no idea why her arm was waving around. She said 'I just felt happy'.
- I influenced a friend to write a particular word 'automatically', by telepathy.

I have used telepathy in an effort to heal people of various ailments. I have had interesting and encouraging results, but will refrain from making any claims. Healing is a subject which deserves a lot more investigation, as also does the word 'faith'.

5: *Two-way Telepathy*

In considering the various aspects of telepathy, it is quite obvious that not all messages are sent or received intentionally. The archives of societies in the field of parapsychology (the study of paranormal phenomena) are filled with anecdotal accounts of people becoming aware of traumatic or death situations, perhaps from the other side of the world. There was no intention on the part of one person to send a message, nor intention to receive on the part of the other. The message could take the form of words, pictures feelings etc., or a combination of many aspects. This phenomenon frequently happens between relatives.

If a dowser can establish a link with a substance, then it

should be possible for someone with adequate sensitivity to establish a relationship with the brains of other people. That, in fact, is what happens when a medium is confronted by a crowd of people at a meeting. The audience usually includes many people, with all sorts of things uppermost in their minds. The medium might, quite unintentionally, 'lock onto' the brain-mind system of a member of the audience which then provides him or her with various pieces of information. The medium does not necessarily understand the 'message', and therefore asks the audience whether someone can make sense of the 'message'.

By deviating a little into the realm of parapsychology (usually known as E.S.P. or extra-sensory perception) I am trying to establish in the reader's mind that Nature, and Nature's creations, including human beings, have far more facets than pure science is prepared to consider. Science always demands proof, proof on its terms. Nature is not always obliging because there are many things in life which cannot be proved. For example, one cannot prove that God does exist nor does not exist. No person can prove his or her love for another person at any given moment. No person can prove to another that he or she is conscious. The most one can do in unprovable situations is to weigh up in one's own mind whether the evidence, plus any instinctive feelings, leads to making a reasonable assumption. By making reasonable assumptions life is made meaningful. We make such assumptions every day of our lives because, without such assumptions, life could not proceed. Assumptions include deciding whether or not a person is trustworthy, or sincere, or capable, or friendly or hostile. We can, of course, be wrong on occasions, but making mistakes is part of the human situation and mistakes have the value of becoming our teachers, and of sharpening our senses.

I hope, by now, the reader is beginning to share my adventure and is able to feel how one thought or one experience leads to another. And if curiosity is part of man's nature, and it is certainly part of mine, then one is literally dragged via one's mind to continue with the adventure. Will such an adventure ever end? – perhaps with the demise of the adventurer concerned, and even that could be a topic for argument in certain quarters. But something useful can be derived, as I have found, from an adventure such as the one I am relating. In fact I have found, as the adventure continues, that everything is inter-related. Ultimately I am hoping that something useful will emerge from all these reports, theories and conclusions, the something that will become a 'model' or basis for understanding human behaviour, including my own. If one can achieve understanding, therein lies the basis of wisdom. As food for thought, a writer once expressed a view that knowledge is as cheap as dirt, understanding as rare as emeralds. Without understanding wise decision-making becomes less likely. Of course it is necessary to realise that not all situations allow for an individual's intervention. Some situations might be beyond a person's ability to make any useful decision other than to accept the situation with simple hope or faith. In writing about my adventure I am concerned about those matters which do allow for decision-making.

Reverting to the topic of E.S.P., as well as decision-making, during the early part of my three years research I reached a point when I began to feel overwhelmed by my experiences and the enlightenment that was beginning to emerge. I felt I had a form of clarity as never before in my life, achieved only by experiments and observations followed by logic and extrapolation. I visited the society for psychical research and took a bookful of my notes to show the secretary – a charming and most intelligent man whose opinions I greatly valued. He read through a lot of my notes, listened to what I had to say, and then informed me that I was in a state of shock as the result of the various findings and revelations in such a short space of time. He also expressed the feeling that what I had written would be believed by only few people, therefore there was not much point in publishing. He felt that most people were not ready for such information. That was nearly twenty-eight years ago, after less than one year's research. What he did suggest was that I should put my knowledge to good use by helping people. That left me wondering what on earth I could do with E.S.P. to help people. Hardly a qualification for a career. I could see no way forward at that time.

Now in writing my original notes I did so in the form of chapters, and I had the habit of clipping together the pages of each chapter by means of a metal staple diagonally across the corner of the top page. What the secretary at the psychical research establishment had said caused me to feel unsure about how to proceed, and whether to publish any findings or not. In discussing my worries with a close friend he suggested that I should consult a medium he knew. The medium might be able to give me some help, he thought. Having never consulted people such as fortune-tellers, mediums and the like, I felt the suggestion was not for me. However, my anxiety put pressure on me and I duly made an appointment with a male medium in London, deciding at the time that I would tell him nothing, hoping he would say something helpful to me.

On arrival I sat opposite to him – a quiet middle-aged man – and he asked what I wanted of him. I said I had a problem and hoped he would be able to tell me something helpful. He asked for my wrist-watch and sat holding it in one hand. He then said, 'I see written papers with pins or staples across the corners, and a shadow across the top of the paper.' He offered no explanation and asked me if I had understood anything. I told him I was impressed with what he had described, and that I was anxious to know whether or not I should publish some findings. He said he could not give me such advice. So apart from the extraordinary description of my papers with the staples, I was still left with my anxiety. But, at least, I had experienced one more phenomenon, namely, clairvoyance, and wondered why it should have been necessary for the medium to hold my watch.

6: *Taking Stock*

Events, experiences, thoughts, some conclusions and theories, came about so rapidly – in a matter of a few months – that it was necessary to pause and take stock, to record some of the more interesting and important details I had to convince myself, to be able to proceed, that what I had done, and intended to continue, would lead eventually to conclusions and understanding of value and help to both myself and others. Consider the chain of events that followed 'the event' with the twig.

I found that other devices for dowsing were being used, namely the bent rods and the pendulum.

Reactions occurred as the result of willing them to occur (subsequently understood to be ideo-motor activity).

I observed that hand movements occurred for reasons other than willing.

I found that dowsing was not limited to seeking and finding water, and that the method could be used in respect of all substances, gases, forces and even for medical diagnosis.

I found a skeleton in a stone coffin, by means of dowsing, with great accuracy.

A question arose in my mind from finding the stone coffin, and the idea of 'domination' resulted. This particular observation is of major importance.

I found that unreliability became a frequent factor in the process of dowsing, involving the dowser's brain-mind system.

Unreliability had to be understood, and I realised that such understanding could only be achieved if a comparison with the methodology of scientific experiments is made.

The last consideration led me to observe that 'constants' are always a feature of scientific experiments. Constants can rarely be part of experiments involving my own brain-mind system, and even less so when observing phenomena derived from the activity of another individual's brain-mind system.

Questions came to my mind as to why humans should display dowsing phenomena.

Those questions led me to see that such phenomena were not limited to humans, but that movements are part of both plant and animal life.

Asking myself why Nature incorporated such things in living creations led me to see the probability that 'survival' is involved.

That in turn gave rise to considerations about survival: that if Nature creates, the creations must have some duration of life, otherwise creation would be futile. In fact without duration there would be no creation. Therefore Nature provides mechanisms for survival.

From the word nature' the word 'supernatural' is derived. I concluded that anything created by Nature, including mechanisms that give rise to unusual phenomena, must be' natural'. Therefore I am inclined to reject the term 'supernatural'.

I concluded that dowsing had to be a form of' telepathy' between a substance etc. and the brain-mind system of the dowser.

I had yet to consider what part the substance itself played in the phenomenon, and what was the significance of a maintained thought of the particular substance. Again a link with 'survival' became a possible answer.

Dowsing itself, linked to the idea of telepathy, gave rise to my further speculations and experiments in connection with telepathy between two individuals.

I also had to consider another important matter, namely that if I could not set up experiments with scientific constants, and I needed 'facts' in order to be able to establish a hypothesis, what could be an alternative? That question led to the realisation that the only option to establish a 'fact' was the process of making 'reasonable assumptions'.

It the became obvious to me that reasonable assumptions had to be made very frequently in respect of everyday life, otherwise life could not proceed and would become meaningless.

I saw clearly that not all things are provable, e.g. the existence or otherwise of God, whether a person is conscious, truthful, loving, reliable, capable, trustworthy and so on. Matters such as those had to come under the umbrella of reasonable assumption, that is to say based upon the judgement of each individual.

In using dowsing devices I observed that hand movements, obviously involving muscles, gave rise to movements of the devices. Then I wondered whether parts of the body, other than hands, might be involved.

The last consideration was dealt with by an unexpected meeting with a young farmer who needed to locate land drains. That meeting resulted in seeing that most parts of the body are probably involved in dowsing.

That in turn suggested that the metal rods might be activated by a change in posture of the dowser's body, leading to destabilisation of the rods.

My general curiosity and virtual obsession for seeking answers to all the questions that came into my mind forced me to associate with many people with scientific and psychological knowledge and expertise, especially a neuro-psychiatrist, and a Professor of Psychology.

The neuro-psychiatrist was instrumental, by virtue of his co-operation, in establishing one example of how a physical effect can be created in another person simply by mental telepathy. I made his nose itch!

That immediately gave rise to considering the possible limits, in terms of physiological effects, which might be produced either in oneself or in another person by thoughts, or by thoughts transmitted telepathically.

In turn I could see the relationship between my previous conjectures and the possibilty of 'healing' by telepathy.

One hears of 'faith healing'; therefore I wondered what is the particular significance of 'faith'.

I have yet to consider the meaning of 'mind', a word used very frequently, yet never properly defined or understood.

My encounter with the professor of psychology, in the form of lengthy and frequent correspondence, taught me one particular lesson, that in order to discuss or argue, one must define the words used in one's arguments. Both parties to an argument must understand and use words with definitions acceptable to both.

Further thoughts about telepathy have led me to see that not all telepathic activity results from a person willing thoughts to be transmitted, nor as the result of another person willing themself to be the receiver of a message. Most telepathic phenomena – recognised usually by thoughts, pictures, or feelings – occur unintentionally. For example, a person might become aware, quite unexpectedly, of some traumatic event occurring which involves a relative or close friend on the other side of the world.

When in a state of anxiety I visited a medium recommended by a friend. Although nothing helpful was said by the medium, the visit did result in my personal experience of clairvoyance, and also made me wonder why the medium needed to hold my watch.

The holding of the watch puzzled me a great deal, and I could only conclude that my watch enabled the medium to establish a powerful link with my brain. So I had to think about the possible qualities which my watch possessed, as distinct from any other watches.

And so on, and so on. The observations, the experiments, the conclusions, the theories – all continued endlessly. Just consider, within this one chapter, what has happened within a few months. Well that is the end of taking stock for the moment. The adventure continues.

7: *Direction Dating and Radioactivity*

Before continuing with reports of further experiences, I must make the reader aware of the fact that my head was literally buzzing with endless questions, with my brain trying to answer those questions by means of experiments. Here are just a few of the questions which nagged away:

How does a pigeon find its way right back home, not merely in the direction of home?

How do cats and dogs achieve the same thing, particularly when they might have been transported in, say, a closed basket over a long distance?

How does instinct work?
What is 'faith'?
What is hypnosis?

Writing down these questions will, I hope, stimulate the reader into having some opinions of his own. One particular thought I had was whether, in addition to substances, electricity, gas etc., I could dowse for 'north' or for forms of time, e.g. to determine the date of something such as a picture or piece of furniture or coins, or even radioactivity, and so on. Again I decided that the only way to find out was by experimenting.

DIRECTION   For 'north' I drove around in my car on a cloudy day without any sign of the sun and did my best to lose myself in unfamiliar territory. Then holding a forked rod (made of cane used in basket work) I slowly rotated until a position was reached when the forked rod started to move upwards. I then checked with a compass. I repeated the experiment on many occasions subsequently, using also the metal rods and pendulum as alternative indicators, and my percentage of successes was very high. In carrying out these experiments I had to take certain precautions – not to guess; to go to locations where there were no observable clues from prior knowledge of the area, nor from the sky; not to be too near any powerful source of electricity because that seemed to affect results; to do the experiments without standing in close proximity to another person. I mention these matters because they stem from my personal experiences.

DATING   I found that by using a pendulum I was able to establish dates of objects, simply thinking of a date in my mind whilst looking at an object. For example, 13th or 14th, or even 20th century. In fact any period if focussed upon in my mind would produce a forward pendulum swing if the correct century was being thought of. If the object did not belong (i.e. was not made) to the period being thought about, the pendulum would not swing directly towards the object, going either at an angle or gyrating. An angle would denote being nearer to the correct period than a gyration. Having, for example, obtained a reasonably positive reaction for say a painting, of the 17th century, I could then continue the experiment by thinking actual dates such as 1610, 1620, 1630 and so on until the pendulum gave a very firm direct swing towards the painting.

This dating of objects became extremely interesting, because it allowed me to look into the windows of antique shops (glass was no barrier) and visually select any item while standing on the pavement outside, holding the pendulum. Obviously the opportunities to date objects were endless, and I had a great deal of fun, and an equal amount of success, with the dating whenever I was in a situation where I could obtain confirmation of a date. The risk was if I were to start guessing or had some prior knowledge of the object. Results would be meaningless in those circumstances.

It so happened that a coin expert placed some Roman coins in front of me, telling me that some were genuine and others were fakes made in the 11th or 12th century. He asked me to use my pendulum to detect which were the fakes. In that instance I had 100 per cent success. I should mention that at that time my 'sensitivity' was at its peak. I was doing experiments 'morning, noon and night'. On another occasion an expert gave me an old chair to examine. First pendulum tests were strange, until upon minute examination with my fingers, while still holding the pendulum, I found that the chair had two dates, because the seat was a replacement for the original, and was therefore of much later date. This particular experience made me realise that it should be possible to detect fakes and repairs in all kinds of objects, including, for example, pottery. I remember checking an old violin and found that the top was 'younger' than the remainder, subsequently confirmed by the owner.

The story of my adventure is, at first, somewhat fragmented, and it will take time to extract the pieces one by one and, ultimately, to join them together to create something more meaningful as the basis for understanding human behaviour. Remember, the first part of my adventure lasted three years, so there is a long way to go before things clarify, unless the reader has already reached some further conclusions. If the reader should embark upon any experiments mentioned so far, then beware not to show off to someone, as it will inevitably lead to guessing or expectation because of your anxiety to prove your ability to the observer, and results will be false.

RADIOACTIVITY   So far as investigations involving Direction and Dating were concerned, the opportunities for experiments were endless. Direction was not, of course, limited to North, and no object was outside the opportunity for dating. However, radioactivity was another matter, but, so it seemed, when one seeks one finds. My involvement in scientific instruments led me to an exhibition of instruments and other laboratory equipment. A particularly friendly stand-holder encouraged conversation with me, during which I mentioned some of the things I was doing with my pendulum. The stand-holder lost no time in issuing a challenge. 'How about radioactivity?' he asked. 'Could you deal with that?' He then produced a wooden block, a few inches square, and about 3 inches or so deep, in which were bored three holes each of about just over half an inch in diameter, like three small wells. He placed the block on the table at a little distance from where I was standing, and told me that at the bottom of each hole was a sample of radioactivity in a small container. He said that one of them was one micro-curie, another was a quarter of a micro-curie and the third was one-tenth of a micro-curie. 'Could you', he asked, tell me by means of your pendulum which is which?' My first reaction was to inform him that I had no idea of the significance of a 'micro-curie', but, since he had challenged me I was prepared to have a go. In brief I succeeded in giving him correct details in just a few seconds, certainly less than a minute, simply by holding my pendulum near to each hole and thinking of each of the possibilities one at a time. The correct one gave rise to the appropriate swing of the pendulum.

I must confess that this was the only experimental situation I ever had with radioactivity, but it does illustrate that the brain-mind system seems to possess knowledge of things we do not necessarily know consciously. Or – could it be that the brain of an individual is part of a network which has connections with all other brain-mind systems in the world? After all, some philosophers do talk of a 'Universal Consciousness or Mind', and similar ideas. Did I, perhaps, pick up the knowledge, unknowingly, from the brain-mind system of the stand-holder?

So it is easy to understand that one event leads to a torrent of questions. That fact forced me to seek ways and means of exploring every avenue with even greater intensity than ever before. First of all I had no income, and was living on capital (not that much), and although I am not a materialist, I had to realise that money was the only commodity to pay the bills for a man, his wife, and daughter. Months were flying by. My close friends were anxious about me and often expressed their concern. 'What' one asked 'are you going to do with all this research to earn your living ultimately?' I replied in all truthfulness I had no idea, but an inner compulsion told me I should not stop.

Through a college in Cambridge I attempted to obtain a scholarship, and although I had been recommended for it by one of the Fellows who was very interested in my activities, I failed to get it. It was awarded to someone who had been working on a history of parapsychology for over twenty years, whereas I had been working at that time on my projects for only about one year, they noted. Although I am not religious in the commonly accepted sense, I do believe in God, and felt, somehow, things would work out.

8: *The Dial*

As the reader may well imagine, to be plunged suddenly into all these activities and their accompanying thoughts, plus a mind-boggling array of experiences which were, to say the least, of a most unusual nature, left me feeling somewhat apprehensive, even anxious. After all, if all my experiences were connected directly or indirectly with my brain-mind system then, I thought, there was the possibility that I might be leading myself up the garden path. Further anxiety arose when a very close friend asked, looking at me very anxiously 'are you alright Harold?' I had no doubt about the implication of his question. In fact my activities were becoming so off-beat that I am sure many of my friends had similar thoughts about me. But I knew I was 'alright', even though I did feel in a kind of shocked state and a little bewildered.

I mentioned earlier that I had some friends with very scientific backgrounds, one being a Professor of Physics. As I was constantly being challenged to prove my claims and reports by means of experiments under 'controlled conditions.' That was the constant demand of each and every scientist with whom I discussed my activities. Otherwise they didn't want to know. By this time I knew they were demanding the impossible, but I also knew that I was involved in matters very much associated with human beings. Phenomena needed to be understood. They could not be swept aside so far as I was concerned. And so I accepted the situation that I had to co-exist with scientific thinking, even though it did not often coincide with my own ideas.

The digs and sceptical remarks expressed by those who think in purely scientific ways produced in me a desire to answer their challenge by seeking some sort of instrument which could be used to indicate reactions of one kind or another. It seemed more scientific, or would look more scientific. But no scientist could offer me such an instrument. Each demanded to know what force or forces I was trying to measure, and I was in no position to give them a satisfactory answer.

Then, because I had spent a great deal of time on dowsing, and had heard of the existence of a society of dowsers, I decided to contact that body. From a conversation with one of their members I found that my experiences were very similar to theirs. That was exciting news for me. The fact that I had researched independently, that I was not influenced by the experiences of others, reinforced my faith in what I was doing. At least I now had no reason to believe that I was misleading myself.

In my desperate search for some kind of scientific instrument I contacted the bookshop near Charing Cross Road where I had purchased the pendulum, and enquired whether they knew of anyone who might be investigating dowsing by means of scientific instruments. The net result of my enquiry was that I was put in touch with a man in south London who was practising what he called 'Radionics' – a branch of dowsing devoted to the diagnosis and treatment of disease. He invited me to visit, and I found him in a small room filled with instruments incorporating large bakelite panels on which were fixed row upon row of dials. We spent the evening in discussion during which he assured me of his many successes in curing not only sick humans, but animals also. I will not attempt to describe his technique. Let it suffice to say I was unable to understand a single part of what he told me, and came to the conclusion that he did not understand it either. He virtually admitted it, but nevertheless had a point when claiming that it did not really matter whether or not he understood what he was doing. What mattered, he said, was that he was making correct diagnoses (confirmed, he claimed, by doctors), and was also making a huge percentage of cures. Furthermore, he rarely saw a patient. He simply worked from a small piece of paper on which was blood, saliva or urine from a patient, sent by post. He treated patients by what he called 'broadcast system' at a distance. Actual distance was irrelevant he said.

I was now feeling almost as sceptical as any scientist would have been, and returned home to brood. Even if, I thought, the system worked, how could I use it if I could not understand any underlying principle. It was not good enough for me. The visit to south London was, however, of some value. Having slept on my thoughts, I woke up the next morning with an urge to possess a dial, even though I had no idea about dials. All I did know was that the dials I had seen were connected to what are called potentiometers. I had also read somewhere that it was thought that magnetism or electro-magnetism might have some place in the realms of dowsing, or so some believed.

Having studied elementary physics about 35 years previously, as a pharmacy student, and having found that subject was not a strong feature of my academic life, I did not anticipate being very intelligent when going into a radio components shop in search of a dial and a potentiometer. As anticipated I was politely asked for specifications. I cannot remember how the decision was made, because I was more than conscious of my lack of knowledge. Eventually I emerged from the shop with a 25 ohm potentiometer, plus an aluminium dial engraved from 0 to 10, and a bakelite knob to act as an indicator on the dial. To go with these items the salesman suggested that I purchase a short length of wire, and a small plastic panel on which to mount the dial. I left the shop with all those things, wondering what I would do with them, and indeed wondering what I expected them to do. Trying to be even more of a scientist I bought a small horseshoe magnet from another shop and made my way home.

Without delay I set about creating my 'instrument'. I connected each limb of the magnet, by means of short lengths of wire and selotape, to the terminals of the potentiometer, set the spindle to the zero position, and mounted all on the plastic panel together with the aluminium dial and knob. I then held the pendulum in my right hand while holding the knob of the potentiometer with my left. The pendulum, which was gyrating, commenced to oscillate in a particular direction. I turned the knob to a new position, and found that the direction of oscillation had changed.

I played with this set-up for hours until I had thoroughly satisfied myself that the setting of the 'dial', as I was now calling it, when changed, altered the direction of oscillation. At last, I felt, I had some sort of instrument! My hopes rose, and during the weeks that followed, my attention and thoughts were centred on the dial. I can tell the reader that, in discussing the dial with some scientist friends, the 'instrument' and the results obtained with it were beyond the realms of their scientific knowledge, they said. So I found myself alone with my dial, but at least I had something with which to work, and to record dial numbers, even though I had no idea of their significance.

One thing I concluded at that time was that the human brain is, in the truest interpretation of the word, a fantastic instrument with enormous versatility. Also, I realised that if scientists do not attempt to subjugate their utter scepticism and prejudice, and refuse to recognise that not all forces can be harnessed for laboratory testing, they will never fathom this miraculous brain which Nature has created. My suggestion to those whose scepticism prevents them from considering old problems in new ways, is to compare any phenomenon which they or their friends have experienced with those reported in this book, to determine whether the explanations which I have written provide possible answers.

Now my thoughts about the dial became more numerous. The fact that different positions of the knob of the dial gave rise to different directions of oscillations of the pendulum fascinated me. I had found previously that just thought of substances gave rise to pendulum swings, each substance causing a swing in a different direction. Logic then led me to see that if the dial, at a particular point of the knob, gave rise to a swing in one particular direction, and a thought of a particular substance caused the same directional swing, then there might be a relationship between a particular dial setting and a particular substance.

It so happened that, in terms of direction, I found that holding a piece of iron made my pendulum swing towards the north. I also found that a particular setting on the dial could also cause the pendulum to oscillate northwards. Even a thought about iron would cause a similar swing northwards. Here, I sensed, was really something worth noting: that there was something in common between a substance, a thought of a substance, and a particular dial setting. Perhaps, I thought, all are interchangeable, so I set about testing the theory.

What I had found from earlier experiments in dowsing was that if I placed two pennies on a table about 12 inches apart, and if I held my pendulum over one of the pennies it would begin to oscillate towards the other. So I used the dial, in conjunction with my pendulum, and set the knob by trial and error to a position based on the thought of 'copper'. When a position was found at which the pendulum was swinging directly towards the dial, that became for experimental purposes, the position for copper. Returning to the set-up with two pennies, I removed one of them and substituted the dial set for 'copper'. I held the pendulum over the one penny, and it began to oscillate towards the dial, as if the dial had become a substitute for the penny made of copper. During further experiments with the dial I found I could relate knob positions, with corresponding numbers on the aluminium dial, for other substances or forces such as water, electricity, bones etc. Each had its own number on the dial.

Another conclusion I reached, following very many experiments, was that in every reaction my brain-mind was involved. I also felt that, at that time, I was pushing myself too hard and decided to pause for a while to give my brain-mind system a chance to digest all that had happened. Another observation was, if a problem proved to be too difficult to deal with at a particular time, by leaving it alone and sleeping on it, it would often become much clearer the following morning. So I never pushed myself too hard in the evenings.

9: *Radionics and Black Boxes*

Experiments with the dial caused me to question the structure of a potentiometer. Without becoming technical I learnt that in essence, it is a length of wire in the form of a coil with an overriding contact which moves along the coil, touching it at various points according to the changes in the position of the knob. I believe it influences how much or little electricity flows, that is if an electrical current was passing through it. In the case of my dial no electricity was involved.

So I thought to myself I would try something simpler to experiment with. I took about 9 inches of ordinary thick iron wire from my garden shed, the galvanised kind, bent it straight and placed it on a table. I then held an ordinary pocket compass about an inch above one end of the wire, and slowly moved the compass along the length of the wire. The compass needle changed its position at various positions above the wire. I knew enough about the earth's magnetic field to recognise that the iron wire was involved with the magnetic field. But, more important, it showed me that the different positions along the wire possessed different properties. So I tested this with the pendulum which I held in my right hand, while touching the wire with my left forefinger. That caused the pendulum to swing in a particular direction. Touching the wire at a different point along its length resulted in the pendulum changing its direction of swing. So here, it seemed, the iron wire was being affected by some field of force, the earth's field, which passed through it.

With the length of wire in front of me I began to think in terms of substances, and found that for each different substance my pendulum would swing towards a particular point along the wire. So now I was establishing some sort of relationship between the thought of a substance and the earth's field.

It did not take long to see that if I bent the wire in the form of a circle, that became a crude equivalent of the wire in the potentiometer. That circle became, as I will tell, equivalent to a card of introduction when visiting another radionics practitioner near Oxford. He made black boxes, so I was told, and had been involved in legal proceedings because of his being accused of fraud. His black boxes, used for radionics, had no scientific meaning or value, was the charge. In short he was found not guilty, was awarded token minimal damages, but had to pay an enormous amount of money for his defence. It was quite a tragedy because he was a very kind and sincere man, and the scientific world, especially in Oxford, wanted to crush him.

It was after this affair that I visited him, and introduced myself by placing my circle of galvanised iron wire before him on his desk. He looked up at me and said, simply, 'So you know'. He then invited me to follow him to his workshop to see his 'black boxes', one of which he opened. Inside was a circle of wire!! Of course his boxes were made in a fairly professional way – they certainly looked so – with dials. He also had special rooms with batteries of boxes with dials which he used for the purpose of diagnosis and treatment of people from all over the world, again by a 'broadcast' system – nothing to do with radio. This was something similar to what I had seen in south London only on a grander scale. So now I had a lot more to occupy my mind. What were the principles or theories involved, I wondered?

From previous experiments I tried to draw conclusions, to establish some principles which might be involved.

(a)   That each organ or system of the body can be related to a position on the dial i.e. has a particular dial number, provided the organ or system is healthy.

(b)   A human sample such as hair, blood, urine or saliva contains 'evidence' as to whether or not a person is healthy, again using a pendulum.

(c)   It seemed to be possible to determine a dial number not only for every organ and part of the body, but also for every part of an organ, and for every known ailment and disease.

(d)   It was claimed that all the dial numbers, if accurately determined, are 'constants', i.e. are the same for all practitioners of Radionics, and therefore such dial numbers can be recorded in a book to be used as a standard reference.

(e)   It was further claimed that it is possible to use dials not only to diagnose disease, but also to cure it.

(f)   That the cure of disease by dials can be effected at a distance e.g. a person in Australia could be treated from Oxford or London or from anywhere else. Furthermore, that it is not necessary to see the patient provided his 'sample' is available.

(g)   That instruments can be made incorporating dials which, when samples are placed in a receptacle, and thoughts addressed to them according to a particular method, can be used for both diagnosis and treatment.

The above notes are a combination of some things I had found out for myself previously together with explanations and claims of Radionics practitioners. I do not wish to confuse the reader by going into further aspects of dials, and the claims some people make for them, but from my own previous experiments it was a most interesting and fascinating period. Certainly the theories, as well as the reactions obtained, deserve more attention than has been given so far. Many aspects remain in my mind waiting to be resolved, if that will be possible. What did intrigue me was that I had discovered a great deal before visiting Oxford, and that some of my own findings had been confirmed independently.

10: *The Bee Knew*

As a change from the technical talk of the previous chapters, it might interest the reader to hear of a most simple, yet thought-provoking, event. I have already told how I was using archaeology as a means of proving dowsing, and that in the course of that activity I dug up many parts of my garden and found pieces of pottery and other items made in earlier times. Therefore I put the word about to neighbours of my special interest, and asked them to let me know if any similar items ever came to light.

Living in the house next door was a delightful elderly lady, a retired headmistress. The caretaker of her former school was a keen gardener, and volunteered to look after her garden on a regular basis. And so it was that on a hot summer's day I looked over the fence and saw the gardener in action. So I called to him, intimating that I would like to come into the garden to see whether I could spot any pottery where he had been digging. 'Of course, come in' he said. (I now know how a robin feels when looking for worms while following a gardener.)

I had a careful look at the places where he had been digging, and felt a little disappointed that I could not find a single item. As it was a beautiful sunny day I took the opportunity to have a short chat with him. We were both standing alongside a waist-high hollow wall, the hollow part having been filled with soil in which colourful flowering plants were growing. As our chat proceeded, a bee alighted on one of the flowers and, almost without hesitation, the gardener swept his hand forward, trapping the bee in his palm which he then cupped with the other hand. So there was the poor little bee buzzing around within the cavity of his cupped hands. Naturally I expressed surprise at what was happening, and the gardener then said: 'If you were to do this the bee would sting you. It will not sting me because it knows I am not afraid. I could trap a dozen or more bees in my hands and they would not sting me'. He then opened his hands and the bee flew off, apparently unharmed.

My inner reaction to this event was not that great at first, but as time passed all sorts of questions, ideas and theories came into my mind. The first observation was that, somehow, the gardener had communicated something to the bee via his hands. What the means of communication was I had no idea. It also led me to ponder about other forms of communication such as via the eyes, as when a dog looks into his master's eyes. Another form of communication could be the pointed finger, as used by, for example, a lion tamer. He would probably use both his fingers and his eyes.

I will leave the reader to think on these matters. Perhaps clues might be found in what I have written previously. But I do feel the incident with the bee is worth reporting.

11: 'Automatic Drawings'

It would be boring, I am sure, for the reader to plough through details of the many thousands of experiments in which I became involved during the first three years of my research. So from now on I will limit my reports to activities which have different features from those previously reported. One such activity was 'automatic drawing', and it occupied many months of work.

As usual, logic came into my thinking. I had observed that thoughts could, among other things, make my hands move involuntarily. That was the basis of the reactions of my dowsing devices. Since, I reasoned, the brain seemed to know a lot of things – such as the whereabouts of materials in the ground – not known consciously, and since the knowledge and thoughts caused hand movements, I considered what else could be discovered about the brain and its contents via one's hands.

Now I have described previously the effect of 'expectation' where the body or the hands are concerned. What is expected consciously leads to the fulfilment of the expectation; it makes it happen. Later in this book I will show how really important is that understanding. So if, in experiments, 'expectation' has to be avoided, it would seem that an experimenter in this field must learn how to

become open minded when attempting discovery. Ana-
lytically minded people usually have difficulty in achieving
this state of mind. The critical faculty dominates, and is
usually based upon past experience. The more past experience dominates the mind, the less opportunity there
will be for discovery.

This prelude to what the title of this chapter suggests,
namely 'automatic drawings', requires me to explain, if I
am able, the meaning of the word automatic. After all,
from everyday experiences it is not likely that the reader
would expect his hands to do something automatically
without, that is, his will and decision being involved.
What I am about to describe are not deliberate, wilful acts.
Automatic in this context means that the writing hand of
the subject, and his arm of course, should be as relaxed as
possible while holding, preferably, a felt-tipped pen. The
only control should be that the arm shall not rest on, or be
supported by, anything. The felt-tipped pen should just
make contact with a sheet of paper, almost as lightly as a
feather, without downward pressure.

The next step was to think of something – for example
'Little Bo-Peep', or a chair, or a fish or any other object
which could become the subject of a drawing. I had to
avoid, as far as possible, any visualisation of the thought.
The thought had to be repeated as words only, silently,
over and over again, at the same time wanting my hand to
respond by providing some sort of drawing without deliberately moving. I simply allowed my hand to do what
it wanted of its own accord. The simplest first experiment
I did was to place the tip of the pen lightly on the left side
of the paper and mentally want my hand to move to the
right, drawing a line 'automatically'. Only by personal
involvement will the reader understand what I mean.
Remember, one must be open-minded, without opinions
or expectations.

At the end of this chapter I show some examples of
automatic drawings, some by people other than myself.

As I stated at the beginning, this automatic drawing occupied months of work. I involved many people, getting them to participate in experiments. Ultimately I found that the brain not only gave information by drawing familiar objects, but also responded in strange ways to all kinds of things such as chemical elements, e.g. thoughts of gold, copper, hydrogen, etc. Drawn 'information' (not always understood) also came about by means of thoughts of e.g. molecules, atoms, electrons, etc. The drawn 'information' tended to change if, for example, thoughts of 'copper molecule or 'copper atom' were used. Once the reader understands by his own experience what is meant by automatic, he will have no difficulty in inventing his own thoughts for exploration.

The matter did not end there. I found, not only by means of my own experiments, but again involving others, that by placing the left hand (for a right-handed person) over an object with the felt-tipped pen in the right hand lightly touching a piece of paper, at the same time mentally wanting the right hand to draw whatever information it obtains from the object under the left hand, the hand will again move and draw automatically. Results can be quite amazing, especially if the object is old, e.g. a piece of Roman pottery, an old photograph or old book. The brain could also request the writing hand to give information in writing as distinct from drawing.

Finally, I also found that drawings resulting from thoughts became affected if the left hand was over the dial. A change in the knob position of the dial affected the drawing. I cannot explain why. I also found that, for many people, if the left hand was over an ordinary magnet, that was likely to increase the intensity of the activity of drawing – things were speeded up – as the result of thoughts.

A SELECTION OF
AUTOMATIC DRAWINGS FROM THOUGHT ·

"woman"
dial 1.0

"woman"
dial 0.45

"woman"
dial 4.0

SOME MORE
AUTOMATIC DRAWINGS FROM THOUGHT

"woman"
dial 5.0

"woman"
dial 2.0

"woman"
dial 2.5

AUTOMATIC DRAWINGS FROM HAND OVER OBJECTS

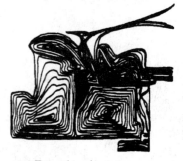

From hand over an
old Victorian photograph

From holding a piece of
Roman Pottery

From holding
an Almanack dated 1754

Further examples of
AUTOMATIC DRAWINGS FROM THOUGHT

"LEAD"   "ARGON"

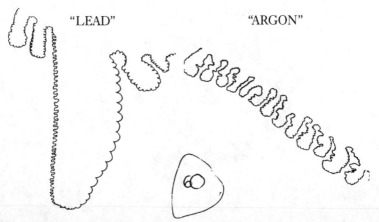

12: *The Brain Apparatus*

Again reverting to dowsing, one observation I made is that the dowser is not in direct physical contact with the object or material being sought. I observed that the reactions occur when the dowser is standing above or in the proximity of what he seeks. A thought that arose from this observation was that perhaps I could dowse over the brain, my own brain. After all, if I could detect electricity in a cable, then possibly I might be able to detect electrical activity occurring in the brain. That is all the electroencephalograph (E.E.G.) does. Why, I thought, depend upon very expensive apparatus when, perhaps, I might be able to obtain equally interesting reactions of the brain by dowsing. I learnt that lesson from the bent rods made for a few pence. To dowse over the brain would, I realised, require an appropriate piece of apparatus.

On the following pages are diagrams of the apparatus I built. First of all I made a skeleton helmet from bent cane. To do that I had to soak the cane (as used in basket making) to facilitate bending. The size was of an easy fitting hat for my head. From the drawings it can be seen that there were many points over the skull where wire was attached – thin plastic covered wire, no electricity involved. Each point of attachment for each wire (there were a total of 91 wires, quite an arbitrary number) was allocated a reference number on a chart. Each wire was long enough to go from the top of my head to one of the 91 points 'switch' on a table in front of me, so that the 91 wires formed a kind of pigtail, and wire was attached, by soldering, to a particular one of the 91 bolts fitted to a bakelite panel. To position the nuts and bolts I had to drill 91 small holes through the bakelite panel, some job I can tell you!!! Each of the nuts and bolts had a reference number corresponding to the point of attachment to the

91-point switch for
BRAIN APPARATUS

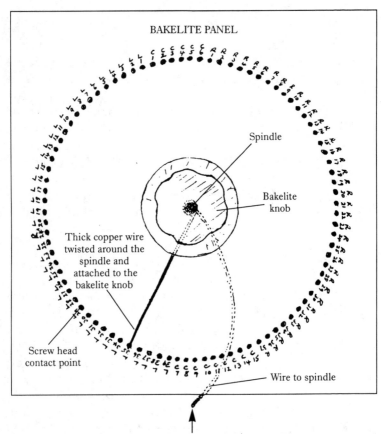

BAKELITE PANEL

Spindle

Bakelite
knob

Thick copper wire
twisted around the
spindle and
attached to the
bakelite knob

Screw head
contact point

Wire to spindle

"Target" for Pendulum

Wiring plan for headgear of
BRAIN APPARATUS

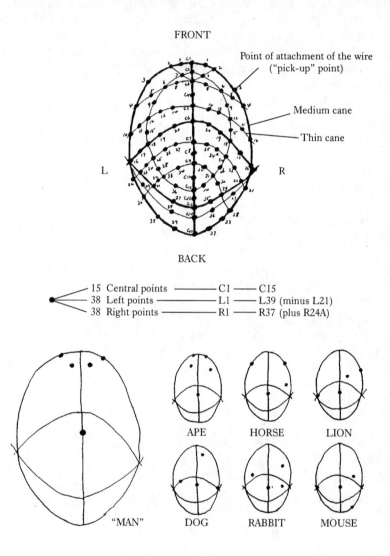

FRONT

Point of attachment of the wire
("pick-up" point)

Medium cane

Thin cane

L   R

BACK

15 Central points ——— C1 ——— C15
38 Left points ——— L1 ——— L39 (minus L21)
38 Right points ——— R1 ——— R37 (plus R24A)

APE   HORSE   LION

"MAN"   DOG   RABBIT   MOUSE

EXAMPLES OF POINTS OF REACTION
BASED ON THOUGHTS

cane helmet. The holes were drilled in a circle, so that another kind of dial was created by fixing a knob, with a pointer attached on a spindle at the centre of the circle. The numbered points on the helmet now corresponded to the same numbers on the dial. It was not necessary for the pointer actually to make contact with the bolts. All that was necessary was for the pointer to be free to ride just above the circle of bolts. When the pointer passed over the head of a bolt it would convey whatever it picked up down the spindle below the knob attached to it, and then from the spindle along another wire, to emerge at the end of the wire in front of the bakelite panel. The end of the emerging wire became the point of 'address' for the pendulum. The pendulum would be the means of detecting whether a reaction was or was not taking place at some particular point within the skull.

The sketches on the following pages show not only the construction of the apparatus, but also illustrations of where, in the skull, reactions took place in response to thoughts. In other words I was now able to dowse over my own head while thinking my own thoughts. Although the reactions were fascinating, I have not yet reached a satisfactory explanation of their full significance. Perhaps in time they will become more meaningful. However, these activities were all part of my exploration and adventure.

13: *What Now?*

As my adventure continued over the first three years, the reader will appreciate how easy it became to be pulled from one direction of research to another and, since in this book I have reported only a fraction of what I did – although I have done my best to mention the most interesting and important experiences – the results, the observations, the theories and the conclusions still represent a puzzle at this stage. There is no 'model' so far in which to incorporate the many findings, to be able to have the helpful knowledge and understanding which comes from a model, as referred to at the beginning of the book.

Just to give the reader an idea of what else formed part of my interest, exploration and work, I will mention just a few in brief:

MAP DOWSING   Fact or fiction? I have reason to think it to be fact. Looking at a map fixed my brain, enabling it to think of other things simultaneously e.g. mineral deposits, oil, etc.

SPIRITUALISM   I offer no opinion. I have no personal experience except as an observer. I do know that I have other ways of understanding how a medium's brain works – explained in a previous chapter.

GHOSTS   I have seen a ghost, the same one, on two occasions. Seeing ghosts is totally subjective, therefore no photographs are possible, while in a soporific state, either just waking up or on the verge of sleep. I believe the source of ghosts to be 'impregnation' of the ground or surroundings by some dramatic event.

POLTERGEISTS   I have had no personal experience. A professor of high reputation has made a study of this subject and assured me they are very factual.

TELEPATHY   How does transmission take place? I wrote a whole treatise on parapsychology which became the reason for my long correspondence with the professor of psychology. In my treatise I postulated the existence of what I called U.F.X. (Universal Field of Force X). This field of force comprises not only the forces known and measured by scientists, but also forces beyond those measurable. All things, thoughts, people, events, exist within that field of force. Any interaction with U.F.X. must produce a 'resultant' force. U.F.X. becomes the carrier, the resultant force is the 'message'. A person's brain-mind system becomes the receiver. Impregnations, previously mentioned, would exist within U.F.X., giving resultant forces.

PREDICTION   If something is a fact, e.g. sliding mud or subterranean movement; or if a thought in another person's mind is maintained and dominating, e.g. an intention to assassinate, then it is quite possible that the brain-mind system of a very 'sensitive' person (the receiver) might pick up the fact, or the dominating thought of intention. That might lead the 'sensitive' to express anxiety, not by actually consciously knowing, necessarily, but by some sort of feeling or apprehension. A process of association is involved.

These were but a few of my interests and involvements. I attended conferences on parapsychology, gave attention to all kinds of paranormal reports; had many discussions with a child psychologist regarding his three year investigation of telepathy in very young children. He reported astounding results, and his research was carried out in conjunction with a university. I also became a member of a society for psychical research, but felt the members were too scientifically orientated to make progress. And so on.
  However impressive, interesting, exciting or any other descriptive term, I or anyone else might apply to my reports so far, the reader, or even a friend is eventually

going to say something, such as: 'So what?' or 'What now?' or 'How does this help me?' as claimed in the prologue. To answer that question I will say simply that a point has been reached where Part I of my book finishes – about the end of my first three exhausting years – and in Part II I will relate the next part of my adventure. I hope matters will gradually become much clearer, and more meaningful, as they did for me.

Part I was not intended to be a treatise on E.S.P. or parapsychology. It was intended only to show how, by studying, or even simply observing, various events and phenomena associated with human beings, it becomes possible quite suddenly to see in everyday things a new significance. I felt that the various phenomena I had observed or experienced were pieces of information communicated by Nature, and it was up to me to interpret them. That was the challenge. Part II includes such interpretations.

PART II

The Following Twenty-Five Years

14: Facing Reality

My adventure had lasted about three years so far, and was not the result of planning. When the twig went up and my curiosity became all-powerful, I had no idea, at the time, what was to come. The effect that initial event had upon me was so great that there was no doubt, in retrospect, that I had shut out from my mind all thoughts of the more mundane side of my life, the side which most people would call reality – earning a living.

Looking back now I can see that most of my previous activities such as pharmacy, philately, numismatics and export were not sources of fulfilment for me. Those involvements provided some interest, and all were sources of learning and earning a living, but I never felt that any one of them gave me the feeling of satisfaction. I felt that there must be more to life than simply devoting oneself to activities for the sole purpose of earning money.

When I was a practising pharmacist, in my early years, I became aware of the fact that drugs and medicines, however useful they might be as 'firemen' from time to time, the problem of health was being approached the wrong way. The promotion of good health, as distinct from the treatment of disease, was to my mind a far more intelligent approach. Why it has taken so long for the promotion of good health to gain ground can, for at least one powerful reason, be attributed to the vested interests of some of those involved in the health 'industry'. I will not enlarge on this point. I am sure most readers will be able to amplify my observation.

However, one thing I did find during my period of

research was that, despite the existence of many influential and important people with whom I had made contact, none had offered me any financial support, neither the academic world, nor private individuals. To be able to keep going for three years required money, and I had managed to put together a small amount by selling stamps, coins and other items from residual stock. Now my money was dwindling, and I reflected upon the advice that had been given to me about two years earlier by the secretary of the society for psychical research, that I should put my knowledge to good use, namely to help people and thereby earn my living. How I would be able to achieve that I had not yet discovered.

At that time my mind had, therefore, two preoccupations. The first was how to turn all the things I had observed, and the conclusions I had reached, into something more practical and, secondly, how to earn some money. Perhaps real need activates the brain, just as the 'fight or flight' mechanism does. So my heightened brain activity led me to see that whatever I had observed, the various phenomena associated with human beings must all belong to one 'model' which would provide a much greater understanding of people as whole beings. So my immediate task became one of assembling the bits and pieces to establish, again by means of logic and extrapolation, a working model.

How it came into my mind I do not know, but I became aware of certain aspects of human behaviour to which I had not given much attention previously, namely being asleep or awake, or any in-between state. The latter seemed linked to the idea of hypnosis, a subject of which I was aware, having seen a stage demonstration and having read several articles on the subject. Being still fascinated by the idea of telepathy, I wondered whether I could induce hypnosis by telepathic means. I had no difficulty in finding willing victims, and did find I was able to hypnotise some people, although I did not fully understand the full significance of the hypnotic state.

Further reflections upon my past experimental work caused me to ponder why Nature had made the various strange mechanisms, for example dowsing and telepathy, to be part of human nature. They were hardly relevant to modern man. Science had provided many more sophisticated and accurate instruments for communication and exploration. Was it, I wondered, that these strange phenomena belonged to the animal kingdom and earlier primitive man? I had already decided that they were provided for survival, but perhaps because of the rapid development of the scientific substitutes for things such as dowsing, telepathy and medical diagnosis, also because of a much more developed thinking process in man himself, the more primitive abilities were either becoming obsolete or were being 'drowned out' by the alternatives.

My final conclusion at the time was that there must be at least two levels of activity in the brain. The lower level embraced all the strange phenomena I had researched and were probably more relevant to animals and primitive man free from the developed thinking and reasoning process as we know it. The higher level is, I concluded, the developed process of thinking and reasoning, the critical faculty, and when the higher level is fully operative, it blocks out the abilities of the lower level which are much more related to 'instinct'.

These ideas were supported when I had discussions with the child psychologist engaged in research in telepathy between young children. He was puzzled by the fact that a high success rate with telepathic experiments occurred with children around the ages of three and four. As their ages increased, so the success rate diminished. The reason was easy to see. As a child grows older he is exposed to more and more information and experiences. That in turn implies that the increase in knowledge in his brain will lead to an increase in the ability to use the critical faculty. The more the latter is used, the more the primitive instincts are blocked out. For exactly that reason the experimenter, or would-be experimenter, in parapsychology (E.S.P.) who continually uses his critical faculty during experimental work becomes just the person who is least likely to experience the phenomena he seeks.

These reflections became the first step in my transition from the realm of parapsychology to ordinary psychology, the means by which, so it proved to be, I would be able to help thousands of people, by sharing with them knowledge and understanding which would enable them to cope with life more easily and effectively. But the story has yet to unfold; step by step everything will clarify. The events of the next 25 years have to be told. The story has to be related as simply as possible for all to understand, not for just a few who use special language and jargon. What a task I see! Nevertheless it will be part of the ongoing adventure.

15: *What to Do?*

My reality, the need to earn my living, became a permanent resident in my mind, with the result that I started to give consideration to everything crossing my mind. The idea of returning to any of my previous activities (except making music, which I did for the love of it only) I dismissed out of hand.

Of all the experiences of the previous three years there was one in particular which attracted me, namely hypnosis. I found it strange when I reflected upon the fact that, at least in the animal kingdom, animals move towards what they need. In extreme circumstances Nature actually leads them. So my being 'led', as it were, towards an interest in hypnosis might, I now think, be loosely connected to the phenomenon displayed by animals. At least it is an interesting thought. It also crossed my mind that, even during my pharmacy days, and from time to time subsequently, the word 'psychology' and all its implications always appealed to me.

During this period I became more aware of the fact that life does not consist of one major activity at a time (certainly not for a married man), that is to say total devotion to one aspect of life with disregard and neglect of all else. Perhaps during the past three years I felt I was back in the student days of my youth. Now my mind, and all the activities going on in it, began leading me to books, magazines and people who were or might be involved in my rising interest in both hypnosis and psychology. Just to clarify, the previous point I made about the similarity between the phenomenon of animals being led and my being 'led' towards particular interests ends when one observes that it is doubtful whether an animal thinks like a human. The animal's response to need arises from what is called 'instinct', and while I know that human beings possess instincts, especially noticeable when observing babies, those are frequently overridden by decisions based on thoughts. In my predicament my actions were probably influenced by both instinct and thoughts.

So I attended conferences on parapsychology, and had many discussions and arguments with academics and others in an effort to clarify at least some of my earlier experiences and thoughts about them, including some of the conclusions I had reached. At one conference I made contact with a professor of psychology of a university in Scotland. He had a 'low profile' interest in parapsychology (it was not regarded at the time as an academic subject, and certainly not scientific), and had a small laboratory which I duly visited. I found the professor's attitude very negative and far too analytical and scientific to be able to achieve results. In the course of quite a long correspondence with him subsequently I was unable to persuade the him to consider any alternative approaches.

At another conference I met a professor of pharmacology from a medical research establishment in the U.S.A. whose special interest was memory. I discussed with him the problems of the scientific method when applied to some phenomena of the brain-mind system. In the course of subsequent correspondence he wrote to me as follows. *I am very willing to admit that the scientific method is not the only valid source of knowledge. It is based on the a fixed relationship between the observing mind and the observed object. When the object is also the human mind (not in the abstract, but an individual mind) the relationship is likely to break down and the scientific method is not applicable any more. This may explain why the phenomena you are interested in cannot be proven scientifically.*

It was certainly comforting to find at least one highly regarded professor who was able to support my view of how unsatisfactory the logic of science is when it comes to understanding the mind of man. I will not hesitate, though, to acknowledge that science has produced miraculous inventions for some of which I have reason to express my gratitude, especially in the realm of medicine and surgery. So I did not take up an anti-science attitude (although some aspects of scientific research are questionable) just to be controversial. I simply felt that there was a kind of arrogance on the part of some scientists to dismiss things which did not conform to their methods of examination as either nonsense, or otherwise inadmissible as facts. Even greater arrogance was when, sometimes, challenged by me to explain some of the phenomena not yet scientifically understood, some scientists would claim that although not understood at present, in the course of time everything would be understood.

Reverting to my interest in hypnosis and psychology, and my increased wish to hear not only spoken words of others but also their writings, I happened to notice an advertisement in a magazine of a lady offering her services as a psychotherapist and hypnotherapist. I took a chance in telephoning her, not to make an appointment, but to discuss how I might be able to learn more about hypnotherapy and psychotherapy. Fortunately she proved to be a kindly person and we had a long discussion during which I mentioned all my previous activities. Being interested in what I had to say, she invited me to her home, and in due course I acted upon the invitation.

The discussion we had resulted in her expressing the view that she considered me to be a suitable person to become capable in the fields of psychotherapy and hypnotherapy, but suggested that, first of all, I should receive some training. I enquired where, or with whom? She suggested a man who had given her a great deal of inspiration and help, not too far from where I lived. By telephone I contacted him and we arranged a meeting at his home. At that meeting he agreed to take me on as a pupil for three months.

The tuition lasted only one month because, and I say this with all modesty, at the end of one month I felt I was able to explain more things to him than he could explain to me. It helped me to realise how much I had learnt and understood about human beings from my three years of research. Nevertheless the one month of tuition helped me a great deal. He insisted that I read books by Freud, Eysenck, Adler and Jung. This I did fairly rapidly because I had no intention of trying to memorise – that has never been my method of learning – what sticks, sticks. The reading did, however, give rise to impressions of the writers' approaches to understanding human behaviour, even though my tutor said he would attempt to destroy much of what I would read.

In brief, lessons consisted discussions of which I was made to make notes. My tutor was a married man with two children, and was an intelligence officer during World

War II. He was about 50, slight built, sallow complexion, with an extraordinary mind. Although calm and soothing in manner, nevertheless had very definite ideas which he put forward in no uncertain manner. He was a believer in straight talk and insisted that hypnosis, E.S.P. and subjects of a similar nature should be considered only on the basis of both feet on the ground. That did not present a problem because it coincided precisely with my own views.

Subsequent lessons dealt with matters such as how to set out a treatment room, techniques for the induction of hypnosis, theories on hypnosis, hypnotherapy, how to conduct consultations, discussions on case histories and the procedures involved. Then, having given my tutor sufficient signs that I fully understood all he had communicated, he arranged for a real patient of his to attend giving me the opportunity to take over the case under his supervision. She was a lady of about 30, a dentist by profession, very tall and overweight. When she binged, usually at weekends, she found she could put on sometimes as much as 10 pounds, and the sessions were intended to help her control eating. Without going into details, all I wish to say is that I achieved satisfactory results, which certainly boosted my confidence in being able to deal with patients. The reader will recall that I used to be a practising pharmacist, so personal contact with the public was not so strange for me.

Further discussions with my tutor included topics such as telephone techniques, telepathic treatment, diversion techniques (especially for children and elderly people), and suggestions for homework to deal with hypothetical cases such as fears, phobias, stress and so on. I will not bother the reader with all the details, because later in this book understanding the brain-mind system and its relationship with the body in physiological terms will become more apparent. In general I can say that as the lessons progressed, I was able to understand more and more clearly most of the underlying processes involved. So it was that my tutor was satisfied after the end of the month that he was unable to teach me more.

What now? Again alone with my thoughts, the first step was to find some patients willing to submit to my therapy, no charge to be made for my services. That was how I started.

16: *Progress*

At this time I was also engaged in vigorous exchanges with two professors of psychology, a child psychologist and a neuro-psychiatrist, all of whom, in one way or another were giving my theories and ideas generally the most intensive scrutiny and questioning. The fact that these people were prepared to engage in such exchanges with me gave me enormous confidence and encouragement, because despite these onslaughts, at no time did I find my theories were threatened.

So it was that I did not exist in some sort of 'ivory tower'. All my ideas were being taken to pieces, and I felt very happy about it. I was in no mood to engage in any form of self-deception. Since that time I have learnt that self-deception is an extremely difficult, if not impossible, task. It is relatively easy to deceive others, but not oneself.

Having made contact with two practising hypnotherapists, and feeling more confident as I succeeded with my patients, my clientele increased, especially as the result of recommendations. With each success my confidence as a practitioner grew. But other things were taking place. I became a member of a group of psychotherapists and hypnotherapists, my admission being dependent upon the submission to their examining board of several case histories and the methods of treatment I employed. Although I have used the word treatment, it was a word I used at the time, but have abandoned since, that is, in the context of my work.

As the result of my membership of the group, in my very early days of practice, I began attending conferences and seminars, all of which gave me further ammunition to destroy any of my self-developed ideas if any new information made that possible. Whilst seminars, maybe, enlarged certain of my ideas, I cannot recall any being destroyed.

One particular series of seminars was conducted at a psychiatric hospital by a psychotherapist who was totally devoted to 'behaviourism', a procedure I disliked the more I learnt about it. I was not hostile to the psychotherapist – each is entitled to his own view – but he was fully aware of my disagreement with most of his procedures. I remember well, and have always laughed about it, how each morning he would greet the seminar group: 'Good morning ladies and gentlemen – and Harold!!'

Although this was something to smile about, it served to remind me that I was, to some extent moving away, at least in mental terms, from many of my friends, who found that they were having difficulty in understanding my concepts unless I went into great detail. My interest in ordinary day to day affairs was being crowded out by all the thinking processes which were taking place in my mind. To me they became far more important than trivial social talk. From time to time an intellectual would engage me in argument (hostility not implied), and to me such activity became the food of life. Some of these intellectuals were highly advanced scientists. One was a professor of physics at a university, another a lecturer in solid-state physics at another university.

One particular problem arose as the result of difficulty with communication. I found that language alone was unsatisfactory simply because a word did not necessarily mean the same thing to all people. Furthermore, some things could be understood only if a person experienced what was being communicated. As an example, because this book, to me, represents the telling of the greatest adventure of my life, essentially an adventure of my mind, I will use the word 'adventure' to illustrate the point. My dictionary gives the following definition of the word: *That which happens without design. Chance, hap, luck. A chance occurrence. A venture or experiment. Chance of danger or loss, risk, jeopardy. A novel or exciting incident. A pecuniary venture, a speculation.* So the reader can see there is nothing very precise or definite about the meanings. One person might choose to emphasise one aspect. Another person a different aspect. If however a person experiences something, including perhaps accompanying feelings or emotions, then only those who have had similar experiences will understand the meaning of the word used to describe the experience. Such are the limitations of language, and unfortunately a person cannot experience everything. Language does not carry within itself the emotions which might be implied.

The dictionary definition of the word 'adventure' really did describe my activities and experiences reasonably accurately. They were multi-faceted. The activities started without design. I took chances – with my capital, my reputation, my friendships. Certainly some luck was involved, especially in making contact with people who put me through my paces. The twig event was certainly a chance occurrence, and for me was both novel and exciting. Eventually one aspect of my adventure has, by necessity, developed into a pecuniary venture. My next chapter evolved from the above considerations.

17: Language, Labels and Communication

At this point I feel it worthwhile to give some thought to many of the 'labels' and language used in this book so far. As just explained, to make a worthwhile communication from one person to another, it becomes essential for the communicator to make sure that any important words he uses shall mean the same to the reader or listener as it does to himself.

To illustrate the problem with labels, that is to say to talk of psychotherapy, hypnotherapy, mind, the brain-mind system, the brain, to name just a few, I wonder how many people could define or explain, again in really meaningful terms, as part of an overall model, any of these labels. Labels are, of course necessary. Certainly a person would not go to a psychotherapist to buy vegetables, nor to a hypnotherapist to have shoes repaired. So labels are necessary, and while they do serve a useful purpose in everyday life, they do not lead to any real understanding when considered in depth. If the term psychotherapist is mentioned, does the reader really believe that all psychotherapists think and work in exactly the same way?

It is not my intention to write the equivalent of a dictionary, so because ultimately I hope to join words as ideas together as a working model, at this stage I will simply engage in providing the reader with an insight into some of the ways my mind has worked in response to a few important words. The reader will understand that a word is merely a symbol which leads to a stimulation of the brain to associate with the particular experience according to whatever is stored in the brain of an individual.

Remember, two people may well have in store quite

different associations with a word. The following are some words for consideration:

SURVIVAL   The first associated thought could be in terms of physical survival. To some it could mean survival of the 'ego' or self. Think of what has happened in the world, and is still happening – the defence of ego in the form of nationalism, religious fanaticism, personal reputations, – leading to wars, social disorder, murder and so on. What humans do to each other for ego survival.

MIND   When in charge of a seminar at a conference, I asked each person present to offer his or her interpretation of the 'mind'. No two people agreed. No person stated anything meaningful. One reason was that the 'mind' is a unique concept, therefore it cannot be described in terms of anything else. It involves a language problem, a communication problem; yet the word is commonly used with great frequency.

'EGO'   Exists because of language. Animals, without the language of humans, have no ego.

BRAIN-MIND SYSTEM   This suggests that it is not brain alone, that the mind is part of a system, of which the brain and its contents are the tangible part, the mind the intangible product of the system, concerned with awareness of some of the contents of the brain.

BRAIN   Without wishing to make too much of the analogy, the brain, an organ of the body, can be likened to a computer, and the information it receives is stored, like introducing computer software. But the analogy ends there. Later in this book the concepts will be dealt with again. Just for the sake of provoking thought, is the brain a separate organ, that is to say, a separate living organ? If the reader thinks it is a separate organ, will he or she say where the organ begins, precisely, and where it ends. In a living being the brain is completely attached and is an integral part of the body, as are all organs integrated to form a whole.

HYPNOTHERAPY   Is this a treatment? Does it (hypnosis) make anybody do anything the hypnotist wishes, irrespective of the individual's wishes? Can one say 'it worked' or 'it did not work'? In any event is hypnosis a thing, or a state of the brain mind system? Some say it is an altered state of consciousness. Altered from what to what? What is implied if a hypnotic state is achieved? These questions will be dealt with later.

PSYCHOTHERAPY   'Therapy' means treatment of disease, or curative treatment. In many psychological conditions there is no disease as such. One is dealing, in the main, with bad 'programming' of the brain. For example, a fear of snakes does not imply that the patient's brain is diseased or damaged. Furthermore, where psychology is concerned, there are many schools of thought, thereby leading to different approaches to problems, according to which school of thought has the greatest influence upon the psychotherapist. Is it possible, I have wondered, whether one school of thought is right, and all the others wrong, or do they all belong to one model?

These mental excursions are intended to represent how my own thinking process operated. None of the ideas expressed are in any sense intended as final statements. They are only intended to be thought provoking, so that the reader can share with me some of the feelings and inner arguments which arose in my mind. One word, as for example, experience can give rise to almost endless discussions, as also the word consciousness. That word has been the topic for discussion and debate between some of the world's top scientists and psychologists. I have attended at least three whole-day seminars on the topic, and by the end of each seminar nobody seemed to have reached any worthwhile conclusions.

While on the subject of words, I feel I must say something about the words 'logic' and 'extrapolation'. These two concepts are important to me because the development of this book has been, from chapter to chapter, totally dependent upon their use as you will see from the following definitions:

'Logic': the branch of philosophy that treats of the forms of thinking in general, and especially of inference and scientific method.

'Extrapolation': the action or method of finding by a calculation based on the known terms of a series, other terms whether preceding or following.

Looking back, all that I have written so far in Part II, and all of Part I, would never have become what it is, a book of mental adventure, if that twig had not gone up in my hand in Leicester Square. But this mental adventure has not yet reached the meaningful objective intended, so I have to relate more in the hope that as I continue, so will the ideas and explanations offer the reader greater clarity and understanding.

I must add that I am, at this moment as I write, feeling a little relieved that I have written so much thus far. It has been exciting for me because it has represented a tidying-up of years and years of work as a professional psychotherapist, during which time I published various findings, observations and opinions, and this book represents the simplest form of a gathering together of what would otherwise be just fragments.

18: *Impregnation*

In chapter 13, under the heading 'Ghosts', I made just a short reference to the word 'impregnation'. It is important that I amplify the word a little for a number of reasons. Firstly it cropped up recently as an implication in a T.V. series called *Heretics* in which the idea was mentioned. It was suggested that substances impregnated or imprinted water to the extent that the imprint did not include as much as even one single molecule of the substance when tested chemically. Nevertheless it was found that the impregnated water seemed to contain a kind of 'record' of the substance which was capable of giving rise to physiological reactions just as if it were the substance itself. The impregnated water was applied to certain animal organs as part of the experiment. The result of this 'heretical' activity was the shunning of the scientist concerned by his colleagues, an example of their fighting for scientific survival. Scientists fear claims of this kind because, if shown to be true, it would undermine the foundations of scientific theories and methodology. It could not be fitted into any known scientific model.

My own views are based on my own experiences, because in the first year of my research, 28 years ago, I found the same effect by accident during dowsing experiments. If, say, a penny was placed on a plate and then removed, for a while after removal my pendulum would react to the thought 'copper', and would swing towards the place where the penny had been. I also found that, while holding an object I could impregnate it with my thoughts.

For example, I put several characteristics of a person by thought into a piece of natural crystal shaped like an egg. While holding it in my hands I thought, for example: tall, fat, blue eyes, fair hair, female, and so on. I put in 10 different characteristics, each one chosen from a group of three possibilities (just like a football pools forecast). Having chosen 'tall', the other possibilities were 'short' or 'medium height'. Having chosen fat, the other possibilities were 'thin' or 'medium build'. I kept a written record of the 10 I had chosen, and on a separate piece of paper I wrote a list of the ten items each having the three possibilities. I placed the egg on a table together with the list of 10 items and the alternatives, and asked a sensitive friend to tell me, by means of the pendulum, which of the characteristics had been impregnated into the egg. My friend announced after a few minutes that he had made a list of his findings, and to my surprise and delight I found he had scored 9 correct out of 10. I can imagine scientists would pour scorn on such a report, and would challenge by their usual method of demanding a demonstration under scientifically controlled conditions.

But this matter still remains important, because the idea of impregnation is the basis of homoeopathy. The original tincture is diluted to such an extent that the final solution does not contain even one molecule of the original substance. Yet the water seems to have been impregnated with its active characteristics.

Finally this topic, impregnation could be the explanation of how dogs, cats, salmon, birds, pigeons, etc. are able to find their way home (their precise base), even over long distances. I am convinced that each animal impregnates its home base and is led by dowsing to the impregnated starting point. It represents 'dowsing for itself'. It is known that birds, for example, navigate by the earth's magnetic field, also by the position of the sun, moon and stars. But Nature often provides alternatives if one or other method fails, as for example on a very cloudy day or night, and I repeat that, from all my observations over many years, I am convinced that impregnation is involved, especially during the final stage of homing, even if the major part of the journey was achieved by other means.

This idea will, I hope, provide the reader with opportunities to create his own experiments and make his own further observations. In so doing I hope one point will always be remembered by the experimenter namely that, when dowsing, you must have no prior knowledge of where the thing you are seeking exists. Knowledge leads to expectation, and expectation produces false results. In conclusion, impregnation probably explains why the medium, mentioned earlier, held my watch. It was impregnated by me, representing a sample of me, which enabled him to establish a stronger link with my brain and its contents (i.e. knowledge and experience recorded there).

19: *Reflections*

When I started to write this book I did say that I felt the task daunting, and that I engaged in the writing because of a feeling of some sort of compulsion. Although I will disclose the fact that I am well past the biblical 'allowance' of three score years and ten (the lady who helps once weekly to keep our house reasonably tidy told me a long time ago that I was living on borrowed time), my feelings about continuing to write are now tinged with a feeling of excitement.

There are many experiences in a person's life, especially when very young, in which excitement is felt when discovering something of beauty or special interest, the discovery being the result of pure chance not cleverness. Such events make the discoverer rush off to tell a friend or relative so that person can share the joy of the discovery. Examples would be a beautiful part of the countryside, an exceptional play or book, the sight of a rare bird or animal, and so on. Of course it is equally conceivable that such a discovery could be used in an attempt to impress others that the discoverer is 'clever'. It is easy to reflect upon how many times in life one is confronted by people wishing to boost their ego, showing off their accomplishments, or by acting or speaking in ways intended to impress.

The reader might have noticed that I have avoided including the names of any people or institutions with whom I have been in contact during the past 28 years. This has been quite deliberate on my part. I have no wish to use any names to support my opinions, findings and conclusions. At my age I can assure the reader the writing of this book is not to fulfil any ambition, nor to seek fame or fortune. I have had all the fulfilment I should expect from the last 25 years as a practising psychotherapist. My instinct is to put my work in an order that will give it meaning to others. It is my hope that the reader will ultimately share with me the understanding which has emerged from the various phenomena and experiments which, although fascinating at times, did not in themselves tell any particularly useful story.

An analogy would be to think of an apprentice to a clockmaker. Imagine that the apprentice is standing before a bench on which rests an assortment of wheels, spindles, springs,, metal parts, small jewels and other metal pieces of strange shape. The clockmaker tells the apprentice that if all those pieces were to be fitted together in a certain way, that would give rise to the creation of a working clock ; that each and every piece needs to be interrelated with the other pieces; that the correct functioning of the clock is dependent upon the correct functioning of each part. If one part should be missing or broken the clock would stop or would not function properly. So it is not difficult to see that this analogy could be applied to the human body, if only the 'components' of the body were as simple as parts of the clock. Nevertheless the malfunctioning of any one part of the body can, as one knows, lead to the malfunctioning of the whole.

Unfortunately, in reality, the clock analogy is not quite appropriate in respect of a human body. In reality there are no separate parts. The whole body is one system, and although labels are put on parts such as brain, kidney, liver, heart etc., those labels are for convenience, especially in surgery, but represent an over-simplification of the body. A further unfortunate reality is that whilst the body itself is tangible, there is one part, namely the brain-mind system, which is intangible. The brain itself is a physical object, but not a separate one in a living body. The mind is not a physical object. The electroencephalograph, and perhaps other instruments, are used to determine the fact that all sorts of activities occur in the brain. Electrical effects can be measured to some extent, but no person has successfully isolated or measured a thought. It is quite intangible, yet thoughts are responsible for an enormous number of physiological effects on the body, such as appetites for food, sex, tobacco and alcohol. Thoughts can, if frightening, cause 'goose pimples', make one's hair stand on end, make one run to the toilet or be sick. The list could be extended considerably.

Therefore it is because the brain-mind system is of such importance – without a working brain a person would be a vegetable – that what I will write in the following chapters will be important. Being important is really an understatement. I will go so far as to say that the brain-mind system of man is far from being completely understood, yet what goes on in the brains of the leaders of countries, of politicians, of even our local doctors, could result in decisions being made which could affect the wellbeing of nations,, localities and individuals. Could there be a more important requirement in life than the understanding of the human brain-mind system?

As I wrote earlier, it is not sufficient to provide explanations in language which becomes jargon understandable only to a small elite percentage of the population. If I have an ambition, which I previously denied, perhaps the reader will excuse one exception namely the wish to lead readers to achieve an understanding of the brain-mind system, and all that is implied, in language that can be understood by any person with reasonable intelligence, irrespective of whether he or she is or was an academic. So for me this is an exciting part of my adventure.

20: *Laying Out the 'Parts'*

So now I am embarking upon what could be regarded as the last mile of a marathon. I am tired, but have got to reach the finishing line, and am feeling rising excitement at the prospect. What follows will amplify some of what has already been said.

THE BRAIN   Tangible. What does it do? A reasonable assumption, arising from the research that has been reported from all quarters, is that information is received by the brain, is stored, then released into the mind from time to time. It also seems to have some inbuilt information which enables it to control various body functions autonomously, that is to say without any conscious decision being made. Examples – blood sugar levels, heart beats, and many more.

MEMORY   One must assume, again by reasonable assumption, that memory is actual awareness of the experiences stored in the brain of a particular individual. One certainly cannot remember what is stored in someone else's brain.

THE MIND   Is the state of being consciously aware, or the

faculty of being able to be consciously aware, of what is stored in the brain.

DOMINATION   So far as the brain-mind system is concerned, domination relates to the fact that one piece of information stored in the brain may have more 'power' than another piece of information on the same topic. The interesting further observation I made was that the idea of domination is not limited to just the brain-mind system, but is applicable to many situations involving people, also animals. It is also applicable to all the senses namely, hearing, seeing, smelling, tasting, feeling and touch. Hence the enormous importance of this particular feature. The reader might recall that this particular idea stemmed from the finding of the skeleton in the stone coffin.

MENTAL NOISE   This is a phrase new so far as this book is concerned. It is a phrase I have coined to explain brain-mind activity. For the brain to record an experience one can understand that some degree of paying attention will be required. How often that phrase was used by my schoolteachers!! If one is supposed to be paying attention, yet at the same time is thinking about something else, if the 'something else' dominates, it will become what I now call 'mental noise', and will prevent the brain of the person from recording properly the matter to which he or she should be paying attention. The brain will, in fact, record the more dominating thought.

RECORDS   If the brain records information in ways which lead to some records being more dominating than others, then the more dominating ones will release information into the mind at the expense of information from weaker records. The information from the latter might not even enter the mind. I wondered why Nature created this system, and reached the conclusion that it was a method for selection. What, I considered, would be a person's mental state if, for example, a word is spoken and as the result every piece of information recorded in a person's brain in connection with the word were to enter his mind at the same time?!!

HABITS   I observed that if the repetition of any activity leads to a 'habit' being created, and if the brain-mind system and its records are involved, the repetition must play some part in the formation of dominating records. Repetition must play some major part in advertising, brain-washing and behaviourism.

IMPORTANCE   The dominating power of a record in the brain is increased if an individual regards a particular experience as being important. So it was a matter that involved each individual's concept of what might or might not be important. From that observation it is easy to understand why people differ so much in the way they conduct their lives. So one can conclude that each person's scale of values is, probably, different from anyone else's in one or more respects.

ACTIONS AND FEELINGS   Both are affected and controlled by thoughts.

NEGATIVE THOUGHTS   These give rise to physiological activities which act in opposition to what might have been activated by a positive thought.

POSITIVE THOUGHTS   Represent the will of a person, that is to say what a person decides to do or stop doing.

TENSION   If negative and positive thoughts in a person both give rise to physiological responses, then if the two kinds of thoughts are activating the body simultaneously, then tension or stress will result.

HYPNOSIS   This is a state of the brain-mind system in which 'mental noise' has been dramatically reduced or eliminated. That in turn will have an effect upon anything recorded in the brain of a person in a state of hypnosis. The state is not, as commonly assumed, one of unconsciousness. On the contrary it is a state in which a person is paying greater attention.

INSTINCT   If a person, or an animal, acts in a way that has no bearing on previously recorded experience, then the brain of that animal or person must contain information which enables actions to be performed without thinking or will being involved. I reached the conclusion – which becomes more and more obvious as one thinks about it – that Nature provides instincts for the survival of living creations, e.g. a baby's ability to suckle, and many similar forms of animal behaviour. A further conclusion can be reached that there must be at least two kinds of records in the brain, one being inherited, the other acquired.

In the next chapter I shall do my best, by assembling the parts, to clarify and express all matters which I consider relevant to enable the reader to understand a great many forms of human behaviour. The only proviso I place upon this statement is that an assumption should be made that the model relates to a brain-mind system of any person whose brain has not been damaged by injury or disease and is not malformed. If the brain has been damaged, then like any machine, it will malfunction according to the nature and extent of the damage, and the model will not be applicable.

21: *The Model*

The brain RECORDS what it receives.

It receives experiences such as things seen, heard, smelled, tasted and touched; also feelings, both emotional and sensual; and thoughts.

The records when STIMULATED, by means of hearing, seeing, smelling, tasting, touching etc., release their information (not always) into what is called our MINDS or our CONSCIOUS AWARENESS. We are able to RECALL and REMEMBER.

Sometimes we are unable to remember some of the information recorded in our brains even though we know it is there. Why does this happen?

If we think of a record as being, in a simplistic way, an ELECTRIC BATTERY WITH A BULB ATTACHED, then a bulb on a battery of say 1000 volts will give a much brighter light than a bulb attached to a 5 volt battery. What is the significance of the BRIGHTNESS; why is it so important?

Just as the light of the sun overpowers or DOMINATES the eyes of an observer, and prevents him from seeing the much weaker light of the stars, so powerful 'lights' in the brain will be the ones first selected from a group of lights (each one of the group of lights representing one particular piece of information about a particular word or topic). If the selected record is extremely powerful it will dominate the other weaker lights of the group, and the information from the weaker records will not be remembered, at least not at that time.

The word POWERFUL, in respect of brain records, is a relative term. If a record is extremely powerful, then that record could be the cause of a PHOBIA, OBSESSION or FEAR. The dominating power will prevent other aspects of the situation from entering the mind, and to allow reasoning to take place. A powerful voltage is created by:

(a) REPETITION – such as HABITS, ADVERTISING, PROPA-
     GANDA, BRAIN-WASHING etc.
(b) GREATER ATTENTION paid to the event the brain is
     recording, implying a REDUCTION OR ABSENCE OF
     'MENTAL NOISE'. Greater attention is usually paid to
     matters which are of IMPORTANCE to a particular per-
     son.
(c) Experiences of CHILDHOOD, because of the absence of
     a developed critical faculty. There is therefore less
     mental noise to interfere during the process of re-
     cording an event in the child's brain.

Why is a record like a battery? Because if a battery is not
recharged eventually, its power will automatically dimin-
ish and the light will become progressively less bright,
just like a FADING MEMORY. The more it fades the less
dominating it will become, and therefore it will have less
influence on a person's thinking process.

So REMINDING is in fact like recharging. For example, if
a person has a powerful record as the result of habitually
(repetitively) smoking, then stops smoking, his smoking
record will fade progressively. However no matter how
much fading takes place, just one puff of a cigarette or
other smokeable object would be sufficient TO RECHARGE
THE RECORD TO A 'VOLTAGE' EVEN HIGHER THAN ORIGI-
NALLY.

If a person is reminded verbally, or by some other
means of some information which might have been for-
gotten, then that reminder will recharge the particular
record of the information which will then be easier to
recall subsequently. But I have stated that one method of
creating a high voltage record is by repetition. That implies that with each repetition the voltage is not only
restored to its original strength, but is made HIGHER THAN
EVER BEFORE. That is what psychologists call REINFORCE-
MENT. The same observations are equally applicable to
drinking alcohol, habits, drug-taking and so on. Once

stopped it must be 100 percent for ever. There can be no compromise once a powerful record has been created.

In the case of OBSESSIONS, PHOBIAS AND FEARS, the initial recordings were extremely powerful because a lot of attention was paid to one frightening experience. Any form of mental re-living of the experience with subsequent avoidance tactics would only lead to the record becoming more and more powerful, totally dominating, that in turn leading to EXPECTATION of unpleasant physiological effects.

We know from school days that repetition enhanced our ability to remember, but what else can be said about PAYING ATTENTION as the means of creating powerful records? I have said that in phobias, obsessions and fears powerful records are in the background. Those records resulted from frightening experiences which, at the time, might have been regarded as threats to physical or 'ego' SURVIVAL. That being important to an individual meant, at the moment of the frightening experience, the individual's brain-mind system was not concerned with other matters, therefore mental noise was absent, therefore a powerful record was created. An example of an important experience would be if a person is in a plane which has to make a forced landing, or if a person is ridiculed in public, which would represent a threat to that person's ego. That in turn might lead to LACK OF CONFIDENCE.

So what is important? Apart from the examples already suggested, the answer depends upon each individual's SCALE OF VALUES. Matters such as pride, education, physical appearance, independence, defects, money, etc. might be regarded by some as being important. On the other hand charity, love, happiness, caring for others, etc. might rate higher in the list of values for other people. All that has been stated so far is concerned with thoughts in the mind or conscious awareness. What has the mind to do with actions and with feelings? Appetites for food, sex, tobacco, alcohol, money, power and so on, are the result of thoughts on those matters i.e. physiological changes have been produced by thought. Equally, thoughts could cause appetites to fade, e.g. thoughts of V.D. could cause the abatement of a sexual appetite.

The movement of limbs is affected or controlled by thoughts. That could relate to all forms of daily activity including domestic, work, social, sports etc. The movement of limbs was dealt with in depth in Part I when referring to dowsing. Remember the farmer dowsing for land drains. Remember also the movement of the hand holding the pendulum. Thoughts were one way of causing the hand to move. However, if a person intends to use a pendulum and at the same time doubts that there will be a response, then the hand becomes rigid and the pendulum will not move.

Previously I referred to positive and negative thoughts. What I have stated above regarding the pendulum is an example of negative versus positive thoughts. Because understanding this mechanism is so important in the daily life of every person, without exception, the reader must understand this matter in every detail. For example, if a bed has to be made, and a person dislikes making beds but nevertheless decides to make the bed UNWILLINGLY, then he has made a positive decision to make the bed, but is simultaneously thinking negatively. His positive thought in action, namely muscles being used to tuck in the sheets, is being opposed by his negative thought in action, being other muscles acting in opposition. In other words any forward movements resulting from the positive thought will be opposed by a backward pull resulting from the negative thought. The outcome of the situation would be that the person would have to use more energy than necessary to overcome the physical opposition created by the negative thought, the bed would be made less efficiently, and the person's body would be in a state of tension as the result of the negative versus positive activity of his brain.

The reader should now consider the situation carefully. The decision to make the bed has been made and will be put into practice. Would the reader consider it a matter of intelligence if a person maintains a negative thought while putting a positive one into practice? By acting in that way will only lead to undesirable consequences, and the bed is going to be made anyway. By removing negative thoughts once a decision has been made, carrying out the decision thereby becomes much easier, the task is performed more efficiently, and no stress is created.

The above simple example illustrates the misleading nature of the expression POSITIVE THINKING. It does NOT mean 'be more positive'. If there is no negative, one does not need to be more positive. All that is required is to be decisive, not impulsively, but based on intelligence and wisdom. Then, having made a decision to do or not do something, simply sweep aside all negative attitudes towards the decision, and put the decision into practice wholeheartedly. Then get into the HABIT OF BEING DECISIVE.

Some of my clients have suggested that removing negative thoughts is far more easily said than done. They say that in theory it sounds fine, but ask how a person can do something not enjoyed, without a negative thought. The simple answer is that probably more than, 90 percent of the things a person does in the course of a day are done because of NECESSITY. A person is indeed fortunate if all the things he does all day are things he enjoys. Top musicians are so lucky! So it is very easy to see to how many situations this principle of negative removal can and should, by habit, be applied every day of one's life. By so doing not only does a person become more effective – at home, at work, in sport, etc., but also ends each day far more relaxed, having done more things in less time with greater efficiency, having used less energy than otherwise. BEING RELAXED IMPLIES BEING THE OPPOSITE TO A PERSON IN A STATE OF TENSION OR STRESS. The latter condition leads to

what are called psychosomatic illnesses such as migraine, asthma, eczema, psoriasis, allergies and many other conditions.

What of hypnosis? I will deal with that in Chapter 23, the next but one. In essence it is a mental state in which mental noise is reduced, allowing more powerful records to be made than would during a situation of ordinary conversation.

In a previous chapter I mentioned that I had reached the conclusion that there must be at least two kinds of records. One type I call INHERITED RECORDS. They are involved with instincts for survival as well as specific bodily features. It is also thought probable that inherited records relate to psychological tendencies as well as latent talents. So far as ACQUIRED RECORDS are concerned, they result from all of life's experiences including the learning process which, so far as the majority of animals is concerned, differentiates them from human beings, most of the former having only a limited learning capacity, usually sufficient for survival purposes.

I do hope that what I have written will be an encouragement to others to observe and think even about trivialities, otherwise the human race will become like some holiday-makers who 'do 14 cities in 14 days'. They run around a lot, but really see very little. But now, although my model has been put on paper, there are more things to say. In fact, as I have said several times previously, this is an adventure which has no actual end. My late father had a saying which I think might be worth quoting. It ran: 'When we are young we think we know everything. When we are middle-aged we realise how much there is to learn, and when we are old we realise how little we know'.

I feel entitled at this moment to pause and reflect upon the enormity, for me, of the changes that have taken place in my brain-mind system as the result of the twig going up in my hands 28 years ago.

22: *Comments from Elsewhere*

Until now I accept responsibility for all that I have written, except for the one quotation about the scientific method made by a professor in the U.S.A., and the quotations from my dictionary about the meanings of a few words.

The Model I have set down in the previous chapter was outlined a few years ago, and I submitted it to a psychiatrist whose opinions and criticisms I have always valued. I will now quote from a letter he was kind enough to write to me:

'– Many thanks for a copy of your Model which I was pleased to read. You ask for comments on it. Neurophysiologically the concepts that you use seem to me to be sound. The relationship between the ability to recall an experience, the number of times that the experience has been recalled in the past and the significance of the experience to the individual have all been shown by psychological studies to be true. Your negative and positive thought analysis is also interesting as there now is considerable evidence that the mid brain neuro transmitter balance can be affected by the thoughts we think and that this in its turn we affect the thoughts which are selected from memory. There is certainly evidence that by altering the neuro transmitter balance, particularly that of the amine system by the use of antidepressant drugs, it will produce a change in thought content and memory selection. So it would seem that your ideas have a sound physiological basis. I can understand that it was difficult for you to promote a discussion, and one reason I am sure is because the topic is extremely complex and the models that we have at the moment are too complicated. Secondly, many members who would read the pamphlet of your model are not themselves familiar with the neuro chemistry which could underpin your ideas –.'

The reference above, regarding my difficulty in promoting a discussion with some members of the psychotherapy group to which I belong, explains why, in the absence of a verbal discussion, I decided to write a pamphlet on my 'model' for the consideration of members, at the same time sending a copy to the psychiatrist for his comments, reproduced above. It is not hard, I am sure, for the reader to imagine how satisfied I felt in knowing that other researchers, following a path quite different from mine, reached conclusions to confirm my findings and conclusions. The difference between the situations arising from researches associated with psychiatry and my own researches, is that the psychiatrists use jargon which is not easily understood by people outside the profession, whereas I have been able to present the same matters in language which I can use for all who come to seek my help.

I will do my best, in the chapters that follow, to clear up as many outstanding matters as possible.

23: *Psychotherapy and Hypnotherapy*

I feel sure the reader will realise that there are really no ultimate statements that anyone can make on the many topics which have been mentioned in this book, without further questions arising, and demands for further or extended explanations being called for. If one were to go to the trouble, I know that it would be possible to trace the existence of numerous books on the various aspects of psychology, as well as on parapsychology, hypnotherapy and science, but also, and especially, on philosophy which is certainly involved in my work.

Therefore I must restate that this offering is not intended to be a textbook. How the reader views or acts upon what I have written is entirely for him or her to decide. My real and earnest hope is that it will promote readers' curiosity, leading to their increased powers of observation, because I have found, as my writings show, that no matter how trivial an observation or event may seem, it could be the means of creating the source of knowledge and understanding. Not all adventures involve travelling. One's back garden could be a source of great interest. Remember how I found ancient pottery fragments and other old artefacts in my own garden which now reside in a local museum.

Because over the past 25 years I have seen, literally, thousands of people coming from many lands, and because most of them came by recommendation, I felt satisfied that what clients had received from me must have had some value, otherwise recommendations would not have continued. That gave me a sense of fulfilment. I have never sought compliments to give me confidence. Results were enough to confirm that my ideas were reasonably sound, and that the expansion of ideas was always based on logic. The important thing about logical progression is to make as sure as possible that any premiss is sound. If it is not, it becomes easy to lead oneself up the garden path.

As a practising psychotherapist and hypnotherapist (labels which do not satisfy me, but are necessary), I feel I must express a few things which I often tell clients, and which I feel are worth stating now.

When people phone for an appointment, in the course of conversation they frequently use the word 'treatment'. They ask how much the treatment will cost, and often add 'Does it work?', or 'How long will it last?', especially when asking for so-called anti-smoking treatment, or when worried about some phobia such as agoraphobia, or fear of flying, or lack of confidence. In response to such questions I am bound to make the matter clear in the minds of clients before they attend, and before I am prepared to see them. When a person uses the word 'it', and sees 'it' as a treatment, that person is implying that 'it', whatever it may be, psychotherapy or hypnotherapy, would lead to the client being absolved from any responsibility for his or her actions. The 'it', they think, will do the job for them, no matter whether it refers to stopping smoking, dealing with a phobia or fear, or say, losing weight. Such clients tend to think that 'it' is worth trying, and if 'it' does not lead the person to achieve his or her goal, then the 'it' becomes the scapegoat for failure.

The reason for this situation is that the public's outlook has been conditioned by the way doctors have practised medicine, and pharmacists (I am still qualified but not practising) have sold medicines. There is always an 'it' for a problem, always a so-called cure for disease.

In fact the practice of medicine and pharmacy have, in the main, been concerned with the treatment of disease, the 'it' being usually a drug or surgery, or both. Neither of the professions have had the promotion of health as their objective. I believe it is changing at last, because I think someone has done a calculation to show that keeping people healthy is more cost-effective, to use a popular phrase, than to treat disease. That consideration does not in any way rule out the use of drugs and surgery whenever really necessary. Those things represent firemen to put out fires. And so it is that an unthinking person sees psychotherapy, and more so hypnotherapy, as a way of treating their problem. Most psychological problems, in people with (literally) undamaged brains have no disease, unless it is psychosomatic, and therefore the words 'treatment' and 'cure' cannot be applied. Since psychosomatic illnesses arise from mental states usually involving frequent negative thinking, if one can improve the mental state and help the client to avoid his own creation of

104

tension and stress, then the psychosomatic illnesses will be cleared up by the body's own healing processes, the latter working much less effectively when a person is in a state of tension..

So what is PSYCHOTHERAPY? It is, in my view, a process of teaching a person how his or her own brain-mind system works, how stress and tension can be created by negative versus positive thinking, instead of employing simple decision-making based on intelligence and free from negative thoughts. Experiments can be introduced to show how the brain-mind system affects and controls all feelings and actions, and how undesirable it is to use words such as 'try', 'determination' and' hope' in situations where such words should not be used. In everyday situations, not calling for any special skill or strength, a simple process of decision-making free from negatives is all that is required. To use the words 'try' or 'determination' in such ordinary situations leads to trouble and failure very often, because both words imply a doubt about successfully carrying out what has been decided.

'Doubt' is, of course, negative. So far as the word 'hope' is concerned, that word should only be employed in respect of matters completely beyond one's control. So when a person has a problem, the first thoughts about the problem should be to decide whether or not the problem is beyond the person's control or intervention, or otherwise. If the problem is beyond one's control, then it has to be accepted, because there is no other helpful decision to be made. When a person refuses to accept what has to be accepted, that is the same as trying to push down the Berlin Wall with one's hands, and is tantamount to fighting the unfightable. In circumstances beyond one's control, it is reasonable to use the word 'hope'.

Regarding HYPNOTHERAPY, the remarks I have made about psychotherapy apply similarly. Hypnotherapy is not an 'it' which removes a person's responsibility for their actions., nor can hypnosis force someone to do or not do something if they do not wish so. Because of stage hypnotism people have strange ideas about hypnosis. They imagine that the hypnotist has complete control over the people involved, and that the people are acting according to the will of the hypnotist, irrespective of their own wishes. I can assure the reader that the people on the stage are willing subjects, otherwise they would not be there. They are carefully selected for suitability by methods employed by the hypnotist, the selection having been made before screening the T.V. show.

The reader might then ask 'if hypnosis will not make me do or not do something why bother to use it; why even be a hypnotherapist?' The answer is simple. For my part it gives me the opportunity to repeat the important parts of what I have said to a client during the previous hour or so.

The repetition of such matters to the client in a state of hypnosis (not asleep) will lead to my verbal repetition being more powerfully recorded than it was during our ordinary conversation. The more powerful records will enable the client to remember the important points of the session. After all, any knowledge, no matter what, is not of much value unless it can be recalled and remembered when required, even though when received it was understood.

I am often asked about EMOTIONS, it being suggested that emotions and thoughts are not necessarily related. I have observed that thoughts precede emotions, and that emotions in their various forms such as anger, crying, hysteria, laughter, and so on, are Nature's method of releasing tension or stress. It is in my opinion most undesirable to instil into a person's mind, especially that of a child, that crying is something that should not be done.

24: The Unconscious, Subconscious and Conscious

These terms are used frequently by people in the course of conversation, and whenever I feel in the mood for a good discussion I challenge someone to tell me what they mean when they use words such as the unconscious, subconscious and conscious. As I said earlier, some psychologists do not accept the word mind. So plenty of opportunities exist for argument and debate. However, I state my interpretation of those terms. Firstly, I consider the brain to be equivalent to a machine (in a very limited sense only) which is not only programmed from birth for instinctive behaviour, but also acquires records from experiences. If a person is unable to remember a particular experience, I would say that the record of the experience is stored in the brain, and that the information in the record has been released by the act of trying to remember (a stimulus). The fact that the person is unable to remember means that the information is being held in an unconscious level of the brain.

Imagine the unconscious level to be a really dark place, so that a person cannot know or 'see' what is there. When the brain is stimulated by any word, situation, smell, sound, situation, etc., the brain's mechanism makes contact with ALL the records associated with the stimulus, but only that record or those records which are sufficiently powerful (of high 'voltage') will cause the information to make its way along, shall I say, a dark passage which becomes progressively brighter as the information's journey continues. At a certain point when the passage has enough illumination to enable the individual to catch a momentary glimpse of what the information might be, but is still unable to identify it, then I would say that the information is in the subconscious. Some people would then describe the situation as 'being on the tip of my tongue'. Eventually when the person's brain activity is quiet, even momentarily free from mental noise, the information is likely to emerge into his mind or conscious awareness. From experience it is well known that information at the subconscious level can and frequently does cause psychological effects, sometimes undesirable, therefore a psychotherapist might feel it necessary to help a client to bring such undesirable information into his mind, or conscious awareness.

What is the mind or conscious awareness in human beings? I am sure that animals have consciousness and are aware of their environment, but I doubt whether, as in humans, they are aware of themselves. They do not seem to be 'self-conscious'. So what is the mind? I can only venture to call it 'conscious awareness', or the faculty of being able to be consciously aware. But because it is a unique mental phenomenon, nobody has been able to describe it satisfactorily in words. Nothing exists to compare it with, so no analogy can be suggested. It is as if another person is inside an individual 'seeing' information released from a record.

So on this debatable issue I think the moment has come to end Part II of my adventure. I feel satisfied that I have 'tidied up my desk', and have brought together a whole heap of matters that have surrounded me for many years. By joining things together and seeing their interrelationship, further ideas and understanding can emerge. I have found that to be so, and I hope the reader will also.

In Part III I am taking the opportunity of keeping my adventure up-to-date by recording a few of the countless thoughts and ideas that pass through my mind from time to time as the result of all my previous and current activities.

PART III

Current Reflections

25: *God, the Scientist and the Smoker*

My view of the scientific method suggests that there comes a point in discussing these matters at which the scientist will not accept any claim unless backed by proof under controlled conditions. So in considering the subject of God, and I do believe in God, I find that where scientists are concerned, demanding proof, there must be a contradiction in a situation where a scientist states he or she believes in God, and I believe that many do. A well known philosopher wrote that one cannot prove or disprove the existence of God, but since it is unwise to act upon unproved assumptions, one should act as if God does not exist unless proof to the contrary comes about.

I am not clear in my mind as to what mental processes take place in the believing scientist's mind that allow for the belief in God, yet cause a complete shut-out of anything else unprovable, such as some E.S.P. phenomena.

While on this topic, I have heard from the lips of many religious people who came to me for help to stop smoking, in reply to my question: 'Do you really want to stop?' the reply: 'Yes, God willing '. I am then obliged to point out at once that if it were a matter of God's willingness or not, they would not need my services. God would make the decision for them. I have to remind people who think in this way that God gave them a brain, for them to make decisions. Therefore they cannot pass the buck back to God.

26: *The Beehive and the World*

One particular reflection that constantly recurs, especially during my work as a psychotherapist is, in the
course of discussions with clients, that I hear of the frequent human situation in which 'man' is his own worst
enemy, individually, nationally and internationally. In
this materialistic world, of which I am a citizen, I have no
escape from the need to earn and possess money as a
means of survival. I learn from clients that many are so
deeply involved in money-making in order to reach a
financial and social level, also to achieve power, that
when that imaginary level is reached it becomes an almost 'I'm alright Jack' concept in their minds. But that
situation, although not expressed by people in such terms,
applies even to a country. Each country of the world is far
more concerned with its own economy and standard of
living than it is with the well-being of other countries,
even though token concern is expressed through United
Nations, Monetary Funds and various charities.

In an earlier chapter I wrote about a bee, and more
recently I gave thought to the relationship between the
bee and its hive. The successful working of the hive is
dependent upon the particular tasks which different bees
in a hive have to perform to maintain viability. Each bee
'knows' its duty and performs it by instinct.

I see this world of ours as a hive, and humans as the
bees. But I do not see a bee as a separate insect. I see it as
a mobile cell as part of the complete hive, the total of the
hive and its bees representing the 'animal'. Therefore if
some of the bees did not perform the tasks required of
them, then the hive would not function properly.

That, to my mind, is what is happening in the world.
The human 'bees', as either individuals or countries are
not working for the benefit of the world as a whole, their

'hive'. Each human 'bee' is more concerned with his own security (material and ego survival). If that happens to help others, that is lucky, if not,' too bad' is the attitude. Of course, this is sweeping generalisation. There are people in the world who, I have no doubt, think as I do, but I feel that they are still a minority.

I am fully aware of how idealistic my thoughts are, and can only hope that wisdom will evolve from self-inflicted human suffering. At least the suffering is a message from Nature that all is not well. I hope humanity will get the message of suffering. It is intended by Nature to create awareness so as to become the means of learning.

My definition of a fool is not a person who makes mistakes, but rather a person who does not learn from them. The final question in my mind on the beehive topic is concerned with the meaning of the words freedom and equality. Can such words be used intelligently if survival is the goal? On what basis can a bee be free or equal if such terms are not compatible with the bee's survival? Perhaps a bee is not hung up on such a human ability as 'the critical faculty'.

27: *Training*

Each human being is unique, even if it were to be so only by virtue of his finger prints. Through scientific investigations it has been found that other physical characteristics can be established as being unique, that is they could only relate to one particular individual. So the individual is unique as a whole. When considering some aspects of individuals, it is easy to see that receptivity in one form or another varies from one person to another, as does learning ability, inclinations and interests, artistic ability as distinct from scientific or mathematic. With each person having variable assortments of those characteristics, especially from an early age when experiences begin to become recorded in a child's brain, some careful thought must be given to the development of an adult if that person wishes to become a teacher.. The teacher should, I feel, possess qualities, sensitivities, which enables him or her to recognise, by a combination of training and instinct, the particular qualities and characteristics of each pupil, and should have the ability to deal with each pupil, to some extent, on an individual basis.

Unfortunately, as I recognise, what I am suggesting is probably not realistic, because running a school, in one sense, is like running a factory or a business, in which methods and rules must be applied to all, not (in the case of a school) modified for the benefit of a select few of the pupils. In the animal kingdom rules are created by Nature's methods and the animals, in the main, (except, perhaps, some domesticated animals), behave instinctively. There are differences in animal characteristics even within a species, but those differences usually lead to establishing groups, with leaders emerging by some sort of domination either of intelligence or physical strength or a combination of both. The rules for living in the animal kingdom are usually, if not invariably, based on survival of sometimes the individual, but more so the species. No special teachers, that is to say trained teachers, are necessary.

If an animal is captured, tamed and then taught to do tricks, as for the cinema or circus, that to me is comparable with behaviouristic psychotherapy, a concept I dislike intensely. Sometimes, when I hear of teacher 'training' I make an association with a trained animal, and feel that that is what such teachers might do to their pupils. I have no doubt that many people share my fears that, because of the large numbers involved of would-be teachers to be trained, and large numbers of students, too much uniformity might result, with disastrous consequences. I cannot be a party (in my mind) to methods of teaching or training which perpetuate the creation of a society whose leading members are so trained as to become dominated by what has been put into their brains, which in turn prevents them from exercising some of their own unique and special abilities, inherent in so many people. In all professions there are always some ordinary practitioners who work by the book, and others displaying the spark of excellence, even genius. It is so important that the proportions within the professions having the mark of excellence shall increase, not decrease because of inferior and uniform methods of training and teaching.

In recording these views I will, of course, agree with any challenge which says, for example, 'I would not like to be operated upon by any surgeon who was not well trained', or 'I would not wish my house to be re-wired by a person who was not well trained as an electrician'. Such views I share. All I am saying is that any form of teaching and training should first of all take into account, in depth, the qualities, talents and skills inherent in each student, and then proceed with training and teaching to a level which does not put the student's brain-mind system into a straight-jacket, but leaves plenty of opportunity for the application of a person's own ingenuity and imagination.

A musician came to me for help. He was a competent player of a wind instrument, and was entirely self taught. However, when he attended recording sessions with other musicians, he often felt inferior to the others because many of them had attended top colleges of music. Having had financial success from playing, he decided he would compensate for his lack 'proper' tuition by going privately to a famous teacher of his particular instrument, and so be able to have first class lessons on technique and other aspects of playing. The net result was that within a week he could no longer play. His brain-mind system was now totally confused by the conflict between his own technique and that imposed upon him by his teacher. I am pleased to say I was able to help him to resume his playing although he had not played for several years.

28: *Faith, Fear and Hypnosis*

'Faith' is a word so frequently used in everyday conversation that I wonder whether the interpretation is the same for everyone. In fact I am sure it does not have just one universally accepted meaning. It is important, however, that clients who seek my help shall have a clear understanding of what faith means.

The word is used in terms such as blind-faith, faith healing, faith in oneself or in someone else, and so on, even in a rabbit's paw. The first observation worth noting is that there is an implication in the word that doubt is absent. Doubt is negative and therefore would act in opposition to any positive thought. So if a person decides to avail themselves of the service (whatever it might be) of another person, a positive decision has been made, but if at the same time there is an absence of faith in the person, then mental conflict will result, including the creation of anxiety and stress. So any person having blind faith in someone or something is, in those circumstances, very relaxed, suffering no stress or tension.

In the case of faith healing, the faith a person has in the reputation of the healer will firstly avoid the creation of stress, and in those circumstances the mental efforts of the healer, and the forces he channels into the patient, will be more effective from a healing point of view. The body of the patient will be more receptive, and healing will be aided by the patient's body also putting into effect its own powers of self-healing which will have been enhanced by the absence of stress.

Fear, on the other hand has some similarity to faith, but in a totally different way. Fear is often associated with a threat to a person by, for example, disease or some hostile action by someone else, or being ridiculed (ego survival threatened). So in the case of fear, a positive thought would be the wish to survive (physically or ego-wise), and the negative one the doubt caused by the threat, again with the creation of stress. But in a state of absolute fear, as in that caused, for example, by witch doctors in their victims, there is no doubt in the victim's mind as to what the outcome will be, namely his death. That is the same thing as being in a state of total expectation. If a person goes to, say, a dentist fearing (expecting) to suffer pain, that person will suffer in real physical terms far more than person who goes having faith in the dentist, and with an open mind on the matter of pain or suffering that might or might not occur.

I have included hypnosis in the title because it too implies the absence of a negative, or at least a severe reduction of it. In a state of hypnosis the critical faculty of a person is reduced or eliminated, and the occurrence of a negative thought is therefore less likely. If the person starts with some faith in the hypnotist, then his words will be even more helpful to the patient.

29: *Young Children and Animals*

As the reader is by now aware, whenever I venture forth to expound a theory relevant to a particular observation, I always feel the necessity to compare other phenomena resulting from the activity of an individual's brain-mind system as evidence in support of my theory. After all, if an observation cannot be fitted within my model, then the model would have to be wrong in at least some detail, or an aspect might have been overlooked. The behaviour of animals and young children confirms my theories.

So when thinking of animals and young children, with the emphasis on young, I think of brains which, in the case of young children, are not full of records acquired from experience, at least much less full than an older child or adult. In the case of animals, all the records are, initially, connected with instincts, even the behaviour of adult animals towards their young. One of my conclusions is, therefore, that in the case of animals and young children, their forms of behaviour could be considered as quite natural in the true sense. Their behaviour is not yet modified by experiences, or if so, very little. Hence a young child is vulnerable in respect of ideas being presented and recorded in its brain. If mother were to say 'the moon is made of cream cheese', a very young child is likely to accept mother's statement as fact, and it would become, if not dealt with, part of the developing critical faculty of the child. Animals are less vulnerable unless domesticated.

One small matter which comes to mind quite frequently is the annoyance I feel when someone says, referring to some undesirable activity of an individual, 'You are worse than an animal'. I feel that is an insult to the animal kingdom from which we humans could learn a lot. Animals have instincts which lead to loyalty, good parenthood, acceptance of responsibility and respectful co-existence, as well as many more worthy activities. They kill usually only for food for survival, and are rarely greedy. Animals also have a sense of discipline, and as with the bees, they act in ways beneficial to their community as a whole.

Young children act and speak as they feel, honestly and without any bias as the result of few acquired mental

118

records. As mentioned earlier, when very young, about 3 or 4 years old, they are quite telepathic, and I recall my own daughter, at around the age of 4, being able to 'communicate' with an old gentleman from Iceland (the father of a friend) who could not speak nor understand a word of English. My daughter knew exactly what he wanted from moment to moment, and he seemed to understand and relate to her with ease. So it seems that two-way telepathy crossed the language barrier.

I also recall the young daughter of a neighbour, about 7 years old, who always enjoyed helping me to keep the plants and bushes, on a roundabout in the road outside our houses, in a tidy state by weeding and clipping. Late one autumn afternoon the sky looked grey, and I had heard a weather report on the radio that rain was expected. So I suggested to my young helpful friend that I appreciated her help, but thought she should now go indoors. She asked 'Why?', and I replied 'because it is going to rain '. 'How do you know?' she enquired. 'Because they said so on the radio' I explained. 'How do they know?' she persisted. 'Because' I said 'they have people looking at the sky and watching which direction the wind is blowing the rain clouds. They said the rain will be coming here'. 'I don't agree with that' she retorted, almost annoyed. 'Why not?' I enquired. 'Because God can change his mind'. What a wonderful example, I feel, of the freedom of expression enjoyed by a child when not tainted by the intellectualism (so-called) of grown-ups.

30: *Food for Thought*

During the course of the 28 years of my mental adventure, I have met many people and heard and read many of their views. Many have stuck in my mind. I think the reader might enjoy reading a few.

'It is necessary to guard ourselves from thinking that the practice of the scientific method enlarges the power of the human mind. Nothing is more flatly contradicted by experience than the belief that a man, distinguished in one or even more departments of science, is more likely to think more sensibly about ordinary affairs than anyone else.

'My view is that medicine may have become too absorbed in treating physical human organisms, and too little concerned with human beings in their homes and their jobs.

'If I had my life to live over again, I should devote myself to psychical research rather than psycho-analysis'.

'When I enter my laboratory, I doff in the cloakroom, with my coat and hat, all preconceived ideas, and allow Nature to speak, in order to find out her secrets.'

Common sense does not necessarily represent being totally aware. It is often the product of self-interest, of one's own opinions, of value judgements and of 'ego' protection amongst other things. It often does not represent wisdom.

31: The Influence of Names

The fact that there is no bibliography at the end of this book is the result of a strong view that I hold. I deliberately avoided putting authors' names to any quotation (not that there were that many), and my reason is directly connected with the functioning of the brain mind system. If I were to look for information of say, a scientific nature, I would certainly look for such information from a person with a scientific background, especially as my own scientific knowledge is limited. Furthermore, the information provided would probably influence my opinions, and any actions I might take as the result. In other words I would pay more attention to the information provided by a scientist on scientific matters, certainly a lot more attention than if a gardener had volunteered information on the same topic.

The same situation would prevail when seeking information on other matters, if provided by a person with a high reputation in a particular field. However, even in realms of science, one particular scientist might be regarded as ranking higher in his knowledge compared with many others in the same profession. Therefore seeking information from a source widely acknowledged as a great authority would obviously lead to being linked with the name of a particular person or group of people. When such so-called authorities speak or write their views or findings, any reader or listener will pay a great deal of attention to the matters expressed. The result of paying so much attention will result in the brain of the reader or listener recording the information very powerfully. The powerful recording will occupy a dominating place, and will greatly influence the individual's subsequent views. That dominance will reduce the person's ability to have access to alternative views which might already have been recorded in his brain, or will influence his critical faculty when alternative views are expressed by people of less authority.

Once a reputation has been established by an individual as being an expert, his utterances will have a profound effect upon the brain-mind systems of people involved in his field of activity. Thus, even before say, reading an article by such an expert, the fact that his name would be attached to the article will lead to the brain of the reader being, as it were, influenced to pay more attention.

I would not disagree with anyone who might suggest

that it is reasonable to be influenced by the views of people who are acknowledged authorities. But the fact is that lesser mortals might speak words of wisdom, or provide information from time to time, even people who might be regarded as amateurs. That in turn will mean that an individual's ability to judge information from unknown or less well known sources might be impaired due to the dominating effect of views of an authority.

My feeling is that I would like to see people able to judge views expressed by less authoritative sources solely on the merits of the views expressed, and not pay less attention to such views simply because of the absence of a well known name. Even ordinary folk and children do utter words of wisdom, and many amateurs have made great discoveries. I would not like to feel that everything in life comes from the mouths of an elite few, having the effect of programming the minds of a population which really has potential to see and think for itself..

The only reason my name is attached to this book is that publications must bear authors' names. I would have preferred to have it published anonymously. The reader should be aware that past history has shown, quite often, that so-called authoritative views have proved flawed; and to have followed an incorrect view on the basis of logic would imply logical progression based on a false premise. One should develop more of an open mind.

If what I have written sounds like the oratory of a politician, then the thinking reader is bound to ask how change can be achieved. I have given this matter consid-erable thought over many years, and have reached a conclusion that change must start in the classroom. There are many subjects taught in schools which lend them-selves to scientific examination, and are classified as sciences. The findings are usually sound, and although, in re-search, some scientific conclusions are challenged, the basis of the scientific method, including its logic and testability, makes challenge difficult, as least by children in the classroom. It is fairly safe for them to accept well proven scientific findings. What could be questioned or challenged is whether some of the products of science are always in the best interests of the human race, as well as planet Earth.

Outside of science there are subjects such as psychology, philosophy, social sciences, art, education, sex, family life and marriage, as examples, which do not lend themselves to totally scientific examination, so that even authoritative views are questionable. All students should be encouraged by their teachers to question and, if necessary, challenge what is taught, so that discussion will ensue. No child or older student should be persuaded to accept statements, even from the highest sources, without being allowed to question or challenge theories, statements and views of academic authorities. No student should have reason to fear taking such action. It would be good for the teachers as well as the students. Sightings of new truths might result.

32: I Wonder

Ever since the event of many years ago I have been aware that something within my brain-mind system became unlocked, releasing a torrent of thoughts, ideas and theories from which I reached some conclusions, including the creation of a model by which some understanding of human behaviour became possible for me. My hope is that what I have written, including the model, will enable the reader to achieve not only a similar understanding of his own behaviour and that of others, but will activate him or her to question, criticise and expand the ideas I have presented, and thereby be able to create an even better model than mine. This is not a book of final statements, but is simply intended to be a starting point for new adventures in the mind of the reader.

Finally I cannot resist from expressing something that keeps going round and round in my mind – I wonder what course my life would have taken if that twig had not gone up in my hands outside the cinema in Leicester Square 28 years ago?

Epilogue

Proof

We all use words in ways well meant
to build and speak our argument,
but when we argue do we know
where and why we're trying to go?

The scientist and the thinking man
says, with information we can plan,
and although it's their intent,
results don't seem so heaven-sent.

Most believe in easing pain
in working less to leisure gain,
to extend the life of man
no matter what is Nature's plan.

And so we all collect the bits, the facts,
    the skills with which one knits
a pattern for society,
knowing in our hearts the truth,
that all that man desires is proof, not
    arguments on deity.

Where does this proof which nags the soul
reside? Because it seems the knowledge bowl
runs over with the things that science finds,
yet leaves us with tormented minds.

Is there something new to seek,
or some new words that man must speak,
so we may freely stand aloof
no longer in the need of proof?

Perhaps the answer can be found
by looking at the things around,

not seeking new, but viewing old
thus might other truths unfold.

Nature is not made of bits
each labelled that it nicely fits,
but is a WHOLE which man must know
before he finds the route to go.